A Devotional

How God Grows a GIRL of GRACE

JoAnne Simmons
with Jodi Simmons and Lilly Simmons

A Devotional

How God Grows a GIRL of GRACE

BARBOUR BOOKS
An Imprint of Barbour Publishing, Inc.

Print ISBN 978-1-68322-322-1

eBook Editions:
Adobe Digital Edition (.epub) 978-1-68322-529-4
Kindle and MobiPocket Edition (.prc) 978-1-68322-530-0

Published by Barbour Books, an imprint of Barbour Publishing, Inc., 1810 Barbour Drive, Uhrichsville, Ohio 44683, www.barbourbooks.com

Our mission is to inspire the world with the life-changing message of the Bible.

Member of the Evangelical Christian Publishers Association

Printed in the United States of America.

06147 0618 DP

DEDICATION

Dedicated in loving memory of Marilyn J. Willett, our beloved Mom and Nana who helped us become girls of grace. With her encouragement, her prayers, her sweet singing, her listening ear, and her gentle love through many joys and trials of life, she never stopped pointing us to the love and hope of our Savior. We miss her dearly, but one day we will be with her again, forever in paradise—all because of Jesus Christ. To Him be all the glory and praise.

INTRODUCTION

Hi! I'm JoAnne Simmons, and my daughters are Jodi and Lilly. I got *a lot* of help from them as I wrote this because they're close in age to you, and God's currently growing them to be girls of grace. Actually, you know what? Even though I'm a grown-up, He's still growing me to be one, too. Anyone who knows Jesus never stops growing in grace, and that's awesome!

I'm praying for you as you read this. I may not know you specifically by name, and I may never actually meet you. (That would be super fun if we did meet, though! We should have ice cream, too! ☺) But I'm positive that God, who does know you by name and counts every hair on your beautiful head, knows if and when you will read this book. He has put you in my mind and on my heart and given me an opportunity to write words to encourage you in your love for Him and your relationship with Him. Will you join me in these devotionals to learn more about how God wants to grow you in His grace and what the Bible says about how we should live?

I pray you find each devotional in this book to be a bit like an icy-cold Popsicle on the hottest, heaviest summer day—cool and refreshing and dripping with sweetness, a supernatural kind of sweetness that comes from the awesome joy of knowing the one true God made *you*, sees *you*, loves *you*, and wants to help *you*, by His grace—with everything!

A DOWNPOUR OF GRACE

Where sin increased, grace increased all the more.
ROMANS 5:20 NIV

Have you ever been mean or selfish toward someone and didn't even say you're sorry, yet the person went right on loving you and taking care of you and giving you good things? Then you know what grace is. Grace is best defined by experiencing it. Good parents, especially, know how to love with grace like that because they learn it from their heavenly Father.

The ultimate, most amazing grace is the kind that God offers. He gives it to anyone who believes that He is the one true God and that He sent His Son, Jesus, to die on the cross to shed His blood to cover our every sin. Not only that, but He rose back to life to be our Savior who gives us eternal life. That's the incredible message of the Gospel! It's because of Jesus' death (that took the place of our sin) and His resurrection (that triumphed over the death that sin causes) that God can offer everyone grace.

God doesn't just offer grace like a little sprinkle, either. No, when we come to Him, He pours it on us like the heaviest rainfall. Have you ever played in the rain? Like you dance with delight in a really good downpour, God wants you to dance in the grace He showers on you. He wants you to know grace and grow in it every day, experiencing His love and forgiveness and His power to help you in all things.

Dear God, even when I don't deserve it, You love and care for me so much anyway. That's grace, and I'm so thankful for it. Amen.

LET IT GO!

Then Peter came to him and asked, "Lord, how often should I forgive someone who sins against me? Seven times?" "No, not seven times," Jesus replied, "but seventy times seven!"

MATTHEW 18:21–22 NLT

If you haven't heard Elsa's "Let It Go" song at least a zillion times in the last few years, then you must have been living under a troll's rock. I might be exaggerating. . .but only a little. ☺ Whether you're terribly tired of the song or happily humming it right now, a great way to apply its three little key words is when you're needing to forgive someone.

Since Jesus offers us so much grace, we are called to give grace and forgiveness easily and abundantly to others. When Peter asked Jesus in the Bible how often he should forgive someone and suggested seven times, Jesus said multiply that times seventy! He didn't mean it in the literal way—that once you get to 490 times of forgiveness you're done and you can hold on to any grudges you want forevermore. He meant it in a way that whatever you're thinking is the right amount to forgive, go FAR above and beyond that and keep on forgiving again and again.

Gracious God, You are so good to forgive me again and again. . .and again. Help me remember this when I need to forgive others. Amen.

SOFTEN YOUR HEART

"If you forgive those who sin against you, your heavenly Father will forgive you. But if you refuse to forgive others, your Father will not forgive your sins."

MATTHEW 6:14–15 NLT

God is so serious about giving grace and expecting us to do likewise that He says in His Word that He will not forgive people who refuse to forgive others. Real forgiveness is not just *saying* you forgive someone, either. It's *acting* like it, too. Ephesians 4:31–32 (NIV) says, "Get rid of all bitterness, rage and anger, brawling and slander, along with every form of malice. Be kind and compassionate to one another, forgiving each other, just as in Christ God forgave you."

Bitterness and anger are often what we hold on to when we haven't truly forgiven someone, and this scripture urges us to get rid of it *all*! Instead of letting our hearts harden up with bitterness and anger, when we truly forgive, our hearts soften with compassion and grace—and gratitude that God forgives us so much. Our heavenly Father has such a soft heart toward us, and we are called to soften our hearts toward others, too.

Dear Father, it can be SO hard, but please help me to fully and truly forgive, letting go of all anger and keeping my heart soft and tender toward those who have done me wrong. Amen.

MAKE IT LOOK EASY

Jesus said, "Come to me, all of you who are weary and carry heavy burdens, and I will give you rest. Take my yoke upon you. Let me teach you, because I am humble and gentle at heart, and you will find rest for your souls. For my yoke is easy to bear, and the burden I give you is light."

MATTHEW 11:28–30 NLT

Grace also means how you handle things or carry yourself. You've probably heard a good ballerina described as having grace. She dances smoothly and beautifully and makes her hard work look easy. Have you ever seen *The Nutcracker* at Christmastime? There are so many graceful dancers and beautiful scenes, and such lovely music!

The grace that God gives is like the word *graceful* describing a ballerina because God's grace *does* help you handle things smoothly and carry yourself well. Being a Christian and having God's grace does not guarantee that everything that happens in your life will be easy and nice, but He will help you handle hard things in smooth and beautiful ways. Also, He will take on the work of each difficult thing and help you make it look easy because you're depending on Him.

Dear Jesus, life can be so hard sometimes, but You give me grace to handle it well. You make things easy for me when I depend completely on You for love and strength. Thank You! Amen.

GRACE FOR THE MESSES

God loves you and has chosen you as his own special people. So be gentle, kind, humble, meek, and patient. Put up with each other, and forgive anyone who does you wrong, just as Christ has forgiven you.

COLOSSIANS 3:12–13 CEV

When Jodi, Lilly, and I were first brainstorming ideas for this very book, we had a funny situation in need of grace. We went to a coffee shop for some treats while we worked together. (Sharing treats always makes work a little more fun, right?) But not long after we sat down, a major spill caused hot cocoa to spread over the table and all down Lilly's pants. She was soaked and had to walk to the restroom looking a major mess in front of a room full of people and then ride forty minutes home feeling quite sticky! We needed grace to handle that situation. Our instant reactions were shock, annoyance, anger, frustration. . .you get the idea. But we all chose to let those first reactions go and instead decided to laugh and make the best of the situation. We focused on the blessings that the hot chocolate wasn't too hot, no one was hurt, and nothing was ruined. We wiped the table, easy-peasy, and the pants washed clean in the laundry! Another blessing was that the baristas gave us fresh hot cocoa!

Let the grace that God constantly gives you fill every single moment of your life so that you can handle anything and everything—no matter if it's a major messy situation or just a minor spill—with a supernatural kind of calm, cool collectedness.

Dear God, help me give grace to others, too, no matter what kind of mess we're in. Amen.

BOLD CONFIDENCE

So let us come boldly to the throne of our gracious God. There we will receive his mercy, and we will find grace to help us when we need it most.

HEBREWS 4:16 NLT

If I ever had the chance to visit the Oval Office to meet the president or Buckingham Palace to meet the queen of England, I'd probably trip over my own clumsy feet, forget what I wanted to say, and nervously laugh too much. What would you do?

What about with God in heaven on His throne? Being almighty Creator God of the whole universe is kind of a big deal. The biggest deal ever, actually! Too many people don't respect Him anymore or even believe in Him at all. That's awful, but it doesn't mean He isn't still the one true God and isn't on His throne, sovereign over all His creation. He's there and always will be, and He'll always be the biggest deal, the one worthy of the most respect and honor and praise. What's so incredible about God's grace is that because of it, you can go to God, not timidly, not with shaking legs and a quivering voice, but boldly to receive even more grace to help you with whatever you need.

Dear God, I am so thankful for Your amazing grace that lets me come boldly to You with anything I need. Please keep growing my confidence in You! Amen.

GETTING TO KNOW GOD

Grow in the grace and knowledge of our Lord and Savior Jesus Christ.

2 Peter 3:18 NLT

Do you know *all* about who God is? No one here on earth knows everything about Him, but a Christian's goal is to keep knowing Him better. He's the best giver of grace, and the more you know about Him, the better you are!

It seems confusing sometimes, but it's important to understand about God that He exists in something called the Trinity, which means three in one. He's God the Father, God the Son, and God the Holy Spirit. He's not three different gods but all the same single God; He just exists in three forms, kind of like there are three forms of water—liquid, frozen, and steam. Their forms don't change the fact that they are all water. That example still doesn't explain the Trinity fully, but it's a start to try to wrap our human minds around the Trinity of God.

When your brain is spinning about God, remember that you don't have to figure it all out! That's the beauty and wonder of faith! Keep trusting that God's Word is true and that His Holy Spirit helps you, little by little, to understand more about Him as you read your Bible and go to church and worship Him!

God, You are awesome and sometimes confusing, too. But I trust You! Please grow me in grace and faith, and help me keep learning more about who You are. Amen.

WHAT'S IN A NAME?

In the beginning God created the heavens and the earth.

Genesis 1:1 NLT

God's many names in the Bible tell us more about who He is and how He loves us. The first Hebrew name of God in Genesis 1:1 is *Elohim*, and it's a name that describes God's power and might and the fact that He is the Creator.

When you're facing something really hard in your life, maybe dealing with a difficult friend or a really stressful situation, stop and think about who exactly you have on your side. *Elohim! Powerful, mighty, and Creator God!* Call out to Him at any and every moment and believe that the almighty God of all the universe sees you, your problems, and your fears and wants to help you. Keep calling to Him, having faith in Him, and waiting for Him to help you in His perfect timing! Romans 8:31 (NLT) says, "If God is for us, who can ever be against us?" And Psalm 118:5–7 (NLT) says, "In my distress I prayed to the Lord, and the Lord answered me and set me free. The Lord is for me, so I will have no fear. What can mere people do to me? Yes, the Lord is for me; he will help me."

Elohim, You are powerful and mighty, and You are on my side!
I praise You and ask You to help me with
the problem I'm facing. Amen.

THE ONE AND ONLY

But Moses protested, "If I go to the people of Israel and tell them, 'The God of your ancestors has sent me to you,' they will ask me, 'What is his name?' Then what should I tell them?" God replied to Moses, "I AM WHO I AM. Say this to the people of Israel: I AM has sent me to you." God also said to Moses, "Say this to the people of Israel: Yahweh, the God of your ancestors—the God of Abraham, the God of Isaac, and the God of Jacob—has sent me to you."

EXODUS 3:13–15 NLT

Yahweh or *Jehovah* is another of the names of God in the Hebrew language. This means "I AM WHO I AM." With this name, God shows that He is the one and only God. There is no one and nothing higher or worthy of all honor and praise!

Is your calendar pretty jam-packed with stuff you have to do? It's hard not to let all the activities and responsibilities and people in your life get in the way of your relationship with God. But it's so important to keep Him first in your life and spend time with Him each day, praying and reading His Word. He is your Jehovah and there is no one else in all of time who is as great as He is, and He wants you to spend one-on-one time with Him every chance you get! How cool is that?

Jehovah, You are truly the greatest, and it's so awesome that You want to spend time with me. Amen.

GOD THE FATHER

You received God's Spirit when he adopted you as his own children. Now we call him, "Abba, Father."

Romans 8:15 NLT

I hope you have a wonderful father in your life, and I'm so sorry if you don't. Either way, you always have your heavenly Father, whom the Bible encourages you to call Abba, which translates like "Daddy."

That means you don't have to think of God like some unapproachable dictator dad in the sky, but you can go to Him with anything. He wants to hug you close and keep you safe, comfort you when you cry, listen when you want to vent, and love you through all of your life. He is so awesome that He's almighty, all-powerful, all-knowing Creator God, worthy of all praise and honor and respect, yet He longs for you to know Him like a cozy and cuddly daddy who wraps you in big bear hugs. Picture your heavenly Father that way. Respect and honor and obey Him, and also bask in the snuggly, warm love He offers you every moment of every day. He never leaves you or lets you down (Hebrews 13:5).

Abba, You're my heavenly Daddy, and I'm so thankful that You're with me and love me so much. Amen.

GOD PROVIDES

"Go into your house with your sons and shut the door behind you. Pour olive oil from your flask into the jars, setting each one aside when it is filled."

2 Kings 4:4 NLT

What a cool miracle God worked through Elisha to provide for a woman whose husband had died and who was about to lose her sons to slavery to pay debts her husband had owed. From one flask of oil, she was able to miraculously fill many, many jars and then sell the oil, earning enough money to pay the debts plus enough for her and her sons to live on.

Just like He provided for this widow, God will always provide what you need, too. One of His names is Yahweh-Yireh (Genesis 22:14), which means "the Lord will provide." Anytime you might be worried for yourself and your family about having money to pay bills or buy food, think about this story and ask God to help you like He did the widow. According to His perfect will and timing, He will make sure you have exactly what you need at exactly the right moment. Trust in His goodness and grace. Trust that He is your constant provider.

Yahweh-Yireh, *You have always provided for me, and I know You always will. Help me to keep trusting You for everything I need. Amen.*

GOD IS PEACE

And Gideon built an altar to the LORD there and named it Yahweh-Shalom (which means "the LORD is peace").

JUDGES 6:24 NLT

The world sure is full of too much fighting, turmoil, and trouble. If you pay attention to the news, you feel like it's everywhere, all the time. That can be so stressful if you let it constantly fill your mind. So don't! Instead, focus on the fact that a name of God in the Bible is Yahweh-Shalom or Jehovah-Shalom. It means "the Lord is peace." He is your constant peace, and He is the only hope for peace for the world.

You cannot possibly control the events of this world or even all the events right around you or in your own home and activities. But you can "do your best to live at peace with everyone" as Romans 12:18 (CEV) urges you. You can't do that on your own, of course. It's far too easy to get into a squabble with someone, especially brothers or sisters, right? ☺ You can only do your best at living in peace with everyone by asking God to help you and believing in Him and depending on Him for true peace. And when you mess up, you can ask God to forgive you, ask for forgiveness from the person you were in conflict with, and then start fresh again, trusting that God's grace covers your mistakes.

Jehovah-Shalom, please steady me always with Your unfailing peace. Amen.

OUR HEALING GOD

"I am the LORD, who heals you."
EXODUS 15:26 NIV

I'm guessing you know someone who is currently struggling or has struggled with cancer or another disease. Maybe they've overcome the disease, or maybe it overcame them. My heart aches for all the loss of our loved ones in this world. In that aching, it's so comforting to know that our God is called Jehovah-Rophi, which means "our God heals." I cry out to God sometimes, "Why, since You can heal here on earth, don't You always do it, and so many people die way too young, and we have to miss them?" When I just can't understand, I trust in the many promises of God, especially that "for those who love God all things work together for good" (Romans 8:28 ESV) and that "the LORD is near to the brokenhearted" (Psalm 34:18 ESV).

Just because God doesn't always answer yes to our prayers to heal someone on earth does not mean He is not the Great Healer. He is. It's just that sometimes healing for a person can only come when they've died here on earth and gone on to heaven, where God provides perfect new bodies that will never, ever get sick. With Jesus as our Savior, we have such a perfectly healthy life waiting for us for eternity, and we trust that our Healer God is good and knows exactly what He's doing.

Jehovah-Rophi, I trust that You care and You heal in Your perfect timing. Please hold me so closely and comfort me when a loved one has gone to heaven to be healed. Amen.

UNCHANGING

"I am the Lord, and I do not change."

Malachi 3:6 NLT

Let's talk ice cream! When I was younger, I couldn't imagine why on earth just plain vanilla was the most popular flavor of ice cream in America. That's still true according to my quick Google search for statistics. I'm *still* not sure how anyone picks ordinary vanilla when they could have soooo many different flavors involving yummy chocolate. Not to mention the fun colorful flavors like Blue Moon and Superman! I could never just pick the same kind of ice cream all the time, especially vanilla, which is good, of course (but so much better with a bunch of hot fudge and sprinkles!). I want variety!

Variety and change in ice cream are great, but I don't like too much variety and change in life. I want some things to remain the same, and yet there's never any guarantee of that. Life can change in an instant in all sorts of ways. That's why it's so important to know that there is one true constant in all of life—God! He is immutable, which means unchanging. Aren't you so glad to know that even if your world turns upside down, God is always the same? He is your rock (Psalm 18:2) and your strong tower (Proverbs 18:10), forever and always.

Immutable God, thank You for being constant and reliable in my life, no matter what is going on or changing around me. Amen.

THE BEST MASTER

I said to the LORD, "You are my Master!
Every good thing I have comes from you."
PSALM 16:2 NLT

Wouldn't it be incredible to find a magic lamp like Aladdin? It's fun to imagine that a genie would have to obey your commands and call you master! What would you wish for?

Do you know that you can call God *Adonai*, which means Master? Using it shows that you acknowledge that you serve and obey Him. Too many people think that's a bad thing, as if you're chained up and treated cruelly like a slave. But that's not true at all with our good and loving Adonai. Serving Him and calling Him Master is an honor and privilege because no one loves you or cares for you more than He does. Every command He wants you to obey that He gives you in His Word results in what is best for you and is full of blessings for you!

Adonai, I trust that You are the very best master and that You only want me to obey Your commands so that I can live the best life possible, the life You created me for. I choose to serve You, and I'm so blessed because of You! Amen.

JESUS, WHAT A WONDERFUL NAME

His name shall be called Wonderful Counselor, Mighty God, Everlasting Father, Prince of Peace.

Isaiah 9:6 ESV

A huge part of the fun of getting a new doll or stuffed animal—or better yet, a real, live pet—is to give it a name! In first grade, I had a hamster I named Reggie. I have no idea now why I picked that name; he just looked like a Reggie, I guess. Too bad I had to give Reggie back to the pet store because he bit me a lot. (That may or may not have had something to do with the fact that I liked to stick him in toilet paper tubes and turn him upside down.)

Ask your parents the story of deciding on your name. Did they know right away, or did it take them awhile to decide? What were some of their other favorites on their list when choosing your name?

When Mary gave birth to Jesus, she didn't name Him herself. His name came straight from God and had been foretold long before He was actually born. Isaiah 9:6 (NIV) prophesied about His name: "For to us a child is born, to us a son is given, and the government will be on his shoulders. And he will be called Wonderful Counselor, Mighty God, Everlasting Father, Prince of Peace." That's a lot of things to call Jesus, right? It helps show us how amazing He is!

Jesus, I don't think I'll ever fully understand how awesome You are, but I want to keep learning more about You every day! Thank You for letting me! Amen.

GOD WITH US

"She will give birth to a son, and they will call him Immanuel, which means 'God is with us.' "

MATTHEW 1:23 NLT

Dreams are crazy things and can seem so very real! I hope yours are mostly good ones and never nightmares. Sometimes dreams aren't great or scary; they're just frustrating. I remember vividly dreaming as a kid that it was Christmas morning, but then I'd wake up and realize it was actually, like, the middle of March, with Christmas still soooo far away. Those dreams sure were mean little tricks my mind played on me, because I adore Christmastime! The presents and decorations and parties are all just so exciting and fun. Every year, though, I fall more in love with Christmas because of Immanuel. That's a name for Jesus that means "God is with us."

Remembering and celebrating the fact that Jesus came to be here on earth with us and knows firsthand our struggles and fears as human beings is so encouraging to my soul. God is with us. God is with *you*. Right now and every moment. No, we weren't alive during Jesus' time as a human on earth, but we trust that He was here and experienced a human life like we are now. And now we have His Word and the Holy Spirit to help us live for Him until our time on earth is up or He returns again, whichever comes first. That's sure a big reason to celebrate at Christmastime—and every other day of the year, too!

Immanuel, You understand me because You came to be a human and lived in this world, too. Please help me to trust You, depend on You, and relate to You more each day. Amen.

LOOK UP TO THE BEST

For God knew his people in advance,
and he chose them to become like his Son.

ROMANS 8:29 NLT

You probably have someone or several someones whom you look up to. Maybe a relative or older sibling or a certain athlete or musician or artist. What is it about them that you admire? It's great to have role models, but remember to keep your head on straight about them. You can respect others and want to have their qualities, too, but there's always a good chance they'll let you down in some way, simply because no human being is perfect.

Only God is perfect, and He sent His Son, Jesus, to become a perfect human being among us. He alone is your only role model who will *never* let you down, and God is asking you to become more and more like Jesus every day. He's your example and guide for how God wants you to live and who He wants you to be like. God knows you can't be just like Jesus all on your own, but His grace covers you and encourages you to keep on striving to live a life like Jesus did, trusting that God sees you as perfect because Jesus took your sins away when you accepted Him as your Savior.

Jesus, You are my best role model.
I want to live my life like You and for You! Amen.

OUR ROCK

The Rock was Christ.
1 Corinthians 10:4 esv

There's a cool place in Florida called Bathtub Reef Beach. Doesn't that sound like you should bring your rubber ducky to swim with? To get there you drive on a road where at one point, you're driving on a strip of land that seems barely any wider than the two-lane road because there is a big stretch of intracoastal water on one side and the vast Atlantic Ocean on the other. Such a cool place! But I couldn't help but wonder how storms and hurricanes don't just easily wash it all completely underwater. There's even a building there called the House of Refuge that's been standing since 1876! It's still intact because the roads and buildings there are built on a rocky shoreline, not just sand. For any structure to endure, it has to be built on something solid—just like Jesus teaches in His parable of the wise and foolish builders (Matthew 7).

You can be sure you're never destroyed by the storms of difficult circumstances if you build your life on the firm foundation of Jesus! Isaiah 26:4 (cev) says, "So always trust the Lord because he is forever our mighty rock."

Jesus, I want to build my life with stability on the firm foundation of You! Amen.

THE HOLY SPIRIT

You know the Spirit, who is with you
and will keep on living in you.
JOHN 14:17 CEV

It's hard when family members and friends live far away. But at least it's easy to keep in touch these days. Jodi, Lilly, and I were talking recently about how in the old days if you missed someone you didn't live close to, you could only send them a letter—and who knows how long it would take to get to them and then get a response back? Sometimes months! Now we have phones, texting, e-mail, FaceTime, Skype, and much faster mail service to keep in touch with people we love when we can't be near them.

Wouldn't it be nice to be able to call, text, e-mail, and FaceTime back and forth with Jesus in heaven? When Jesus was ending His time on earth, He knew we all would miss Him and wish we could communicate directly with Him, and He said, "I will ask the Father to send you the Holy Spirit who will help you and always be with you. The Spirit will show you what is true" (John 14:16–17 CEV).

Until we get to heaven, Jesus did not leave us alone. The Holy Spirit, who is fully God, is here with us. In the Bible, He is called our Helper and Comforter and Advocate.

Holy Spirit, I believe You are right here, right now.
Please remind me of Your presence constantly,
and help me to learn to depend on You for everything. Amen.

GOOD WARNINGS

"The Holy Spirit tells me in city after city that jail and suffering lie ahead."

Acts 20:23 NLT

Do you ever get a bad feeling about something that you can't quite explain? I'm not talking about just a bad feeling that putting brussels sprouts in pudding is probably gross. I'm talking about times when you have a serious vibe that you need to avoid a situation. That can be the Holy Spirit warning you of danger or trouble, like Luke was warned in the book of Acts.

I've had several experiences in my life when I thought I should avoid a situation or a decision. Sometimes they didn't make much sense other than just kind of a sense that something wasn't quite right. Our world often just calls it a gut feeling, but the Bible shows that the Holy Spirit can sometimes be the source of those gut feelings. Ask God to help you have wisdom and discernment. Our world is full of so much confusion and sin and untrustworthy people that it's absolutely necessary for Christians to constantly be praying for the Holy Spirit's help in avoiding danger and making good choices.

Holy Spirit, I need Your guidance all the time! Please give me wisdom and discernment. Amen.

Beautiful Boldness

After this prayer, the meeting place shook, and they were all filled with the Holy Spirit. Then they preached the word of God with boldness.

Acts 4:31 NLT

If I could travel in a time machine, back to my younger self, I'd do it and I'd grab my own shoulders and shake them a little and say, "Be more confident!" I spent way too much brainpower worrying about messing up and what other people thought of me.

So much of my lack of confidence in my younger days probably came from fear of being made fun of and fearing the future wouldn't turn out well. But that means I was trusting too much in myself rather than in God. The Bible says that "the Spirit God gave us does not make us timid, but gives us power, love and self-discipline" (2 Timothy 1:7 NIV).

Don't let this world and your worries steal your confidence. Always remember that you are a daughter of the King of all kings! Let His Holy Spirit fill you and inspire you to be beautifully bold.

Dear God, help me to have confidence that is based on You. Amen.

BOLD BUT NOT TOO BOLD

Not to us, O Lord, not to us, but to your name goes all the glory for your unfailing love and faithfulness.

Psalm 115:1 NLT

You do have to be careful with boldness. There is such a thing as too much, and that can cause some seriously obnoxious or annoying behavior. You have to balance boldness with being wise and humble—and wanting all glory and praise to go to God and not to yourself.

Nobody really likes to interact with people who seem to think they know everything. Sometimes people with too much boldness come across that way, and it's called arrogance. When I was in school, one of the most annoying things EVER was when one particular student raised their hand to answer every single question and pretty much never let anyone else have a chance to participate in class discussion. A good teacher will notice that and not let just one student overtake the class, but it's still annoying when they try.

Ask God to make you bold and outspoken when He wants you to be, and also ask Him to show you when it's better to just be quiet and listen to others. There are times for both.

God, I need Your help knowing when to speak out for You and when to just quietly listen to others whom I want to share Your love with. Help me be bold yet humble and do everything for Your glory. Amen.

FORGETFUL FOLKS

"But the Advocate, the Holy Spirit, whom the Father will send in my name, will teach you all things and will remind you of everything I have said to you."

JOHN 14:26 NIV

I am forever misplacing things around the house—especially forgetting where I last put my phone. One time I even put it in a basket of laundry I was carrying downstairs. . .and then I dumped the whole basket in the washing machine and washed my phone along with the load of whites. The bad news was it was totally dead; the good news was that it sure came out of the laundry squeaky clean!

Do you forget where you put things like I do? Or maybe you forget a certain chore you're supposed to do each day or the homework you leave in your backpack.

John 14:26 shows us that God understands that we are forgetful folks. He gave us the Holy Spirit to both teach us and remind us of all the things Jesus said. He knows we need constant encouragement and reminders of truth. How hard it would be to keep on track with God's Word in our culture today if we didn't have the Spirit constantly encouraging us to remember it!

Holy Spirit, thank You for teaching me and reminding me of all that Jesus said. It's so good to have You with me all the time. Amen.

TRUE OR FALSE?

"And I will ask the Father, and he will give you another advocate to help you and be with you forever—the Spirit of truth."
JOHN 14:16–17 NIV

If you ever follow the news these days, you'll hear about fake news and false accusations and a constant need for fact-checkers. It seems like every day it gets harder and harder to know what's really true and which people are safe to trust! Thankfully, the Holy Spirit of God who is with us at all times is called the Spirit of truth. He can constantly help us determine what is true and what is false, whom we can trust and whom we need to be wary of.

John 16:13 (NIV) says, "But when he, the Spirit of truth, comes, he will guide you into all the truth." Don't let the world discourage you with so many lies. Trust completely that you have God's Spirit to show you truth in all things. Let Him guide and direct you every step of the way.

Spirit of truth, thank You for guiding me and showing me what to believe. I would be so lost in lies and confusion without You. Amen.

DON'T GIVE UP ON OTHERS

For it is God who works in you,
both to will and to work for his good pleasure.
Philippians 2:13 ESV

Do you have someone in your life you keep inviting to church but they just won't come? Do you have someone in your life you keep praying for that they will want to know and love Jesus, but nothing seems to change?

Don't give up! It's your job to simply share the love and truth of Jesus as the Holy Spirit guides you. It's never your job to force someone to accept Jesus as their Savior. Only God can truly soften a person's heart to want to know Him. As you wait, keep praying and don't lose hope. Read Jeremiah 24:6–7 (NLT) and pray that God does the same for your loved ones who need to know Him as He said in that scripture: "I will watch over and care for them, and I will bring them back here again. I will build them up and not tear them down. I will plant them and not uproot them. I will give them hearts that recognize me as the Lord. They will be my people, and I will be their God, for they will return to me wholeheartedly."

Dear God, please help my loved one want to know You.
Please care for and protect them and draw
them close to You. Amen.

GOD MAKES THE SEED GROW

I planted the seed in your hearts, and Apollos watered it, but it was God who made it grow.

1 Corinthians 3:6 NLT

As you keep praying for a friend or loved one to come to know Jesus, remember that God can use others in their lives to draw them close to Him, too. Read what Paul says in 1 Corinthians 3: "Who is Apollos? Who is Paul? We are only God's servants through whom you believed the Good News. Each of us did the work the Lord gave us. I planted the seed in your hearts, and Apollos watered it, but it was God who made it grow. It's not important who does the planting, or who does the watering. What's important is that God makes the seed grow. The one who plants and the one who waters work together with the same purpose. And both will be rewarded for their own hard work" (1 Corinthians 3:5–8 NLT).

Have faith and confidence that it's never all just your job to lead others to Christ! It's your job to keep walking closely to God and letting His light shine through you and His love be given through you. Ask Him each day how He wants you to do that.

Dear God, thank You that all of us who love and serve You are working together to share the Gospel. I pray for my loved ones who don't know You that they will receive the Gospel! Amen.

UNIQUE GIFTS

There are different kinds of spiritual gifts, but the same Spirit is the source of them all. There are different kinds of service, but we serve the same Lord. God works in different ways, but it is the same God who does the work in all of us.

1 Corinthians 12:4–6 NLT

I bet your friends have a lot of the same interests as you, but I bet you're very different, too. That's part of the fun of being friends. You learn and grow and enjoy one another because of differences. How dull our world would be if everyone were all the same!

The Bible talks about how God's Holy Spirit gives different gifts to each of His people, different ways to serve Him, different ways to help one another. God has blessed us all with unique talents and individual abilities to do what He asks us to do. How cool is that? It's so important to never compare and expect other Christians to be exactly like you. God purposefully made you and every other person different, with tasks specifically designed for you. Let Him show you what they are, and then do them for His glory!

God, thank You for my unique gifts. Help me to know how and when to use them like You want me to. Amen.

ONE WITH MANY

The human body has many parts, but the many parts make up one whole body. So it is with the body of Christ. Some of us are Jews, some are Gentiles, some are slaves, and some are free. But we have all been baptized into one body by one Spirit, and we all share the same Spirit.

1 CORINTHIANS 12:12–13 NLT

The human body is incredibly fascinating! Do you enjoy learning about it in your science classes? God is an amazing Creator. It's mind-boggling to think about how so many different parts work together so well to make you a living, breathing, thinking, feeling, loving, active, working, talented, creative human being! But when all our different body parts don't work together in the way they're supposed to, that's when we get sick.

Now, think about how Paul describes God's people, the Church, as one body with many parts. We have to realize and appreciate that we're all very different, with unique spiritual gifts and jobs to do. If we don't do that, the Church gets sick and doesn't function well, either. We have to be willing to celebrate the differences and work together in unity like a healthy human body.

Dear God, please help me to appreciate all the differences in Your people, and help me work toward unity in Your Church. Amen.

POWER IN WEAKNESS

Be strong in the Lord and in his mighty power.
Ephesians 6:10 NLT

You have unique strengths and talents, and you have unique weaknesses, too—things that are harder for you than they might be for other people. We all do, and we shouldn't be ashamed of them. Did you know the Bible says you should actually be happy about them? Sounds a little crazy, I know, but it's true, and here's why: When you're really good at something, you don't have to ask for help with it, right? But if you can admit you can't do something on your own, you know you need help. If you realize that you need to depend on God in those areas where you struggle, then you'll get closer to God because you'll keep asking Him for His help. He'll be so happy to assist, and you'll grow closer and closer to Him as He gives you the strength and ability you need! Second Corinthians 12:9–10 (NLT) says: " 'My grace is all you need. My power works best in weakness.' So now I am glad to boast about my weaknesses, so that the power of Christ can work through me. That's why I take pleasure in my weaknesses, and in the insults, hardships, persecutions, and troubles that I suffer for Christ. For when I am weak, then I am strong."

Dear God, no matter what weaknesses I have, remind me that You have the power to help me with anything! Amen.

SHEEP IN WOLF CLOTHES

Many false prophets have already gone out into the world, and you can know which ones come from God.

1 John 4:1–2 cev

There are some *seriously* confusing kinds of differences among churches and people who call themselves Christians. Some differences are no big deal because they're just a matter of traditions and different tastes. But some differences result from churches and teachers and preachers going against the Word of God. Second Corinthians 11:13 (cev) says these false teachers "only pretend to be apostles of Christ."

God is not surprised by these false teachers and churches. The Bible warns us again and again about them. But we don't have to be afraid. Plant yourself firmly in Jesus, and through the Holy Spirit, He will help you discern or figure out the false teachers and churches from the ones that truly know, love, and serve Him and that preach the whole Word of God. It's all about their fruit! Matthew 7:15–20 (cev) says, "Watch out for false prophets! They dress up like sheep, but inside they are wolves who have come to attack you. You can tell what they are by what they do. No one picks grapes or figs from thornbushes. A good tree produces good fruit, and a bad tree produces bad fruit. A good tree cannot produce bad fruit, and a bad tree cannot produce good fruit. Every tree that produces bad fruit will be chopped down and burned. You can tell who the false prophets are by their deeds."

Holy Spirit, please keep me on the lookout for false prophets, and help me avoid them. I want to hear what You want to teach me, straight from Your Word and Your leading! Amen.

DON'T JAM IN THE JUNK

For a time is coming when people will no longer listen to sound and wholesome teaching. They will follow their own desires and will look for teachers who will tell them whatever their itching ears want to hear. They will reject the truth and chase after myths. But you should keep a clear mind in every situation.

2 Timothy 4:3–5 NLT

Back in Bible times I'm guessing they didn't have Doritos and Kit-Kats and Sourpatch Kids and Skittles. We have a lot more junk food these days that we have to be very careful not to fill our bodies with. We also have a lot more junk for our brains available everywhere we go. Movies, books, TV shows, music, magazines, a zillion different websites and blogs. There's a lot of good stuff out there in the media, and a lot of really awful stuff, too.

I think people make it harder and harder to listen to the Holy Spirit by filling their minds so much with the junky things of this world. I know I'm guilty sometimes! That's why in such a confusing world with so many false teachers, it's more important than ever to be extra, extra, *extra* careful what we watch, read, and listen to, and what activities we participate in. God is always so near through His Holy Spirit, but how much do we tune Him out by the junk we keep jamming into our brains?

Dear God, help me empty my mind of the things that aren't good for me. I want to keep my mind clear so that I can easily hear from You. Amen.

HIS FOLLOWER FIRST

So don't boast about following a particular human leader. For everything belongs to you—whether Paul or Apollos or Peter, or the world, or life and death, or the present and the future. Everything belongs to you, and you belong to Christ, and Christ belongs to God.

1 Corinthians 3:21–23 NLT

You definitely need leaders in your life who help you grow and mature. Your parents are your first leaders, and as you get older, more people come into your life to help teach you and guide you. You might have favorite teachers or coaches or music instructors. Your most important leaders are the ones who point you to a good relationship with Jesus Christ and help you grow in it. The Bible warns about never boasting about following any of these leaders, though. You have to be careful to never hold them up too high because any human is able to fall from a position of good leadership. Let Jesus alone be your one best leader whom you're always looking up to and getting guidance from in His Word and through the Holy Spirit. Yes, you have parents and teachers and others who want to help you and teach you good things, and you need to listen to them and obey. But most of all you belong to Jesus. You are His follower first and foremost! He knows you better than anyone else and wants to lead you in the very best kind of life!

Dear Lord, You are my very best leader, and I never want to stop following You! Amen.

HELP FOR THE FIGHT

You, dear children, are from God and have overcome them, because the one who is in you is greater than the one who is in the world.

1 John 4:4 NIV

No doubt, we have enemies in this world. The Bible says, "Your enemy, the devil, is like a roaring lion, sneaking around to find someone to attack" (1 Peter 5:8 CEV). He is the god of this world, but he is nothing like the one true God with a capital G! We don't ever have to fear, for within us is God's Holy Spirit, and as 1 John 4:4 says, He is greater than the one in the world. The Holy Spirit gives us the power to overcome the devil and any enemy or hard circumstance that comes against us.

Dear God, You are great and mighty—so much greater than the devil and all the evil of this world! You are with me and You protect me. I have nothing to fear because with You I can overcome anything Satan and this world throw at me. Amen.

HOW TO PRAY

Likewise the Spirit helps us in our weakness. For we do not know what to pray for as we ought, but the Spirit himself intercedes for us with groanings too deep for words.

Romans 8:26 ESV

Do you ever just feel like you're stuck with a mouth full of Laffy Taffy when you're trying to pray? You don't ever have to feel bad about that! It also doesn't mean you should just stop praying. God definitely wants to hear from you, and He wants you to tell Him your every worry and need, for others and for yourself, but the Bible says you won't always know what to pray for as you should. Thankfully, the Holy Spirit intercedes, or does it for you, with groanings that are too deep for words. That means the way the Holy Spirit communicates our prayers is in a way that is just too much for us to fully understand. But God understands! He sees all and knows all, and nothing surprises Him. He cares about your every need.

Holy Spirit, thank You that when I'm not sure how or what to pray, You are doing it for me. Amen.

THE LORD'S WAY

"Our Father in heaven. . ."
Matthew 6:9 ESV

Jesus gave us some clear instructions on how to pray. You've probably heard of the Lord's Prayer. It comes from the scripture in Matthew 6: " 'When you pray, don't babble on and on as the Gentiles do. They think their prayers are answered merely by repeating their words again and again. Don't be like them, for your Father knows exactly what you need even before you ask him! Pray like this: Our Father in heaven, may your name be kept holy. May your Kingdom come soon. May your will be done on earth, as it is in heaven. Give us today the food we need, and forgive us our sins, as we have forgiven those who sin against us. And don't let us yield to temptation, but rescue us from the evil one' " (vv. 7–13 NLT).

That's some very straightforward instruction from Jesus! It's a great idea to memorize this prayer and keep in mind its guidelines. When you pray:

- Praise God
- Pray for His will to be done
- Ask God for what you need
- Ask for forgiveness and help in forgiving others
- Ask for protection from temptation and from the enemy

Lord, thank You for understanding I need help with knowing how to pray and for teaching me in Your Word! Amen.

LEAVE IT UP TO HIM!

"But you will receive power when the Holy Spirit has come upon you, and you will be my witnesses in Jerusalem and in all Judea and Samaria, and to the end of the earth."

ACTS 1:8 ESV

You want to tell others about Jesus and His love, but it can be scary sometimes, too, right? Just remember that you know the hope of the world, the best news EVER that Jesus loves people and died and rose again to give us eternal life. And don't worry about when and how you will share with people. Just keep close to God and leave it up to Him! Keep praying for His will to be done in your life, and tell Him you are willing and able to share His love with others whenever He wants you to. Then let Him show you how and when He wants you to share with others about His wonderful love and salvation. God's Holy Spirit will give you the words and actions you need if you are walking closely to Him and are staying sensitive to His leading.

Holy Spirit, please keep me constantly aware of Your presence, and help me pay attention for the times when You want me to share with others about Jesus' love and grace. Please use me for Your will. I know You will help me with everything You ask me to do. Amen.

PLAIN AND SIMPLE

Always be prepared to give an answer to everyone who asks you to give the reason for the hope that you have.
1 Peter 3:15 niv

I like big words, but I'm glad the Bible tells us we don't *have* to know them. It does tell us we always need to be ready to share with others about why we have hope (1 Peter 3:15), but it doesn't say we have to do that using elaborate speech with a big vocab. In fact, the apostle Paul talked about how he purposefully did *not* use fancy words sometimes when teaching people about Jesus, and he even talks about how he was super nervous and trembling with fear at first! (That makes me feel so much better because I'm such a big chicken about speaking in front of big groups of people!)

Read what Paul said in 1 Corinthians 2:1–5 (cev): "Friends, when I came and told you the mystery that God had shared with us, I didn't use big words or try to sound wise. In fact, while I was with you, I made up my mind to speak only about Jesus Christ, who had been nailed to a cross. At first, I was weak and trembling with fear. When I talked with you or preached, I didn't try to prove anything by sounding wise. I simply let God's Spirit show his power. That way you would have faith because of God's power and not because of human wisdom."

Dear Jesus, help me to just share simply and honestly about how awesome You are! Amen.

THE WORD

In the beginning was the Word, and the Word was with God, and the Word was God.

John 1:1 NIV

God is constantly with you through His Word, the Bible. He didn't physically write it Himself, but He used regular people to record the inspired words He gave them. Second Peter 1:20–21 (NLT) says, "Above all, you must realize that no prophecy in Scripture ever came from the prophet's own understanding, or from human initiative. No, those prophets were moved by the Holy Spirit, and they spoke from God."

Why can you trust the Bible as God's Word? you might ask. If you took time to study the origin of the Bible, you would find that scholars and archaeologists have discovered time and time again that the Bible is accurate and consistent throughout history. Not to mention all the people throughout history whose lives have been transformed because of the Bible! And most importantly, there were so many eyewitnesses to the miracles of Jesus and to the fact that Jesus died on the cross then rose back to life! He is worthy of your trust and so is the Bible.

Dear God, thank You for Your Word that I can trust and read anytime I want to hear from You! Amen.

BIG DECISIONS

All Scripture is inspired by God and is useful to teach us what is true and to make us realize what is wrong in our lives. It corrects us when we are wrong and teaches us to do what is right.

2 TIMOTHY 3:16 NLT

Do you ever hear people say, "I just wish God would tell me exactly what to do!" when they are struggling with a big decision to make? I know I've said that before myself. Maybe you have, too! We wish God would speak to us directly whenever we need Him to. The thing is, He does speak to us all the time, through His Word. If you spend consistent time learning about Him and reading the Bible, He gives you everything You need to know to live a good life and make wise decisions. You have to keep the whole Bible in mind, though, not just the parts of it you like best or that sound the nicest. That's why it's so important to keep God first in your life, make it a major priority to go to church where the Bible is studied and preached thoroughly and accurately, and not just hear the Word but *do* it—live it out! Those are the ways God best communicates to His children, and you are one of His treasured children!

Dear God, I want to listen well to Your Word. Please help me understand when it seems confusing. Please help me to be consistent in learning more about You and Your Word! Amen.

OUR GOOD SHEPHERD

"I am the good shepherd. I know my own and my own know me, just as the Father knows me and I know the Father; and I lay down my life for the sheep."

JOHN 10:14–15 ESV

Have you ever watched the show *Dirty Jobs* with Mike Rowe? He needs to travel back in time and do an episode with the shepherds in the Bible. They sure didn't have a glamorous job! It was dirty and smelly and seriously hard work. Yet Jesus called Himself our Good Shepherd. He is certainly no arrogant, fancy-pants master of His people. He's our King of all kings and the Lord of all lords, yet He didn't demand a palace or anything special during His time here on earth. No, He is humble and so good to us, walking with the poorest of people and healing and performing miracles to show us the way to God. He put our needs before His own. He is our leader, yet He serves and cares for us, too. That's the very best kind of leader. He's such a good shepherd that He gave His life for His sheep. He gave His life for *you* to be saved.

My Good Shepherd, You lead and care for me so well. I will always follow You! Amen.

LIGHT AGAINST DARKNESS

God is light, and in him is no darkness at all.

1 John 1:5 ESV

Jodi, Lilly, and I attended a stargazing event at a nature center in Florida recently. We got to peer through some big telescopes and learn about several different constellations, and we saw the planet Venus shining very brightly. God's creation of all the stars and galaxies is beyond amazing! Of course, it had to be dark outside in order to see the stars. The darker the better, actually.

Sometimes when I get discouraged about how dark our world seems to be getting with sin growing so popular and being flaunted all around us, I remember that light shines brighter in darkness. And Jesus said, "I am the light of the world. Whoever follows me will not walk in darkness, but will have the light of life" (John 8:12 ESV). When we know Jesus as our Savior and we have the Holy Spirit with us, we are shining His light on a very dark world. And when we learn and live by and share God's Word, we spread God's light, too, for the Bible is a lamp for our feet and a light to all our paths (Psalm 119:105). So don't get discouraged by darkness. Use it for opportunities to shine God's light in your life brighter than ever before!

Dear Lord, please help me to shine brightly for You in a dark world. Amen.

NEVER ALONE

I am with you. Don't tremble with fear. I am your God. I will make you strong, as I protect you with my arm and give you victories.

Isaiah 41:10 CEV

You go for years as a baby and then a little girl when it's not safe to be home alone because you don't quite know enough to take care of yourself. No one should leave a little child all by herself before she's ready! And then suddenly you reach the age (maybe you're there or are almost there) when now you do know enough about safety rules and such that you can be left alone at home for certain lengths of time. Maybe you love that kind of independence or maybe it scares you a little—or maybe even a lot. If it scares you, be encouraged that God promises time and time again that He is always with you and is protecting you according to His perfect will. Call out to Him for comfort when you feel lonely and afraid. Talk to Him at any time, out loud even when you're home alone. Treat Him like He is right there in the room with you, because He always is! And if you enjoy the independence and it doesn't scare you at all, still never forget that He is with you. Enjoy the time alone when you can better focus your thoughts on God's constant presence with you!

God, remind me that You are here with me every moment of every day. Amen.

WHEN YOU'RE NOT ALONE BUT LONELY

Do what is right and good in the LORD's sight.
DEUTERONOMY 6:18 NIV

Sometimes the worst kind of loneliness isn't when you're truly all alone; it's when you're surrounded by people but you feel like you just don't fit in and maybe you're afraid of being teased or laughed at. Or maybe you took a stand among a group of friends to avoid something you feel is wrong, and the rest of your friends chose to participate anyway. I know exactly what that's like, but I look back now and I'm thankful for those times. That seems crazy when you're young to be thankful for awkward social situations where you feel like no one understands you and you have no one to talk to and no one to stand up with you for what you believe in. But if you let those hard moments make you stronger friends with Jesus and hold tighter to His Word, then that's the part to celebrate!

In a world where so many people go along with anything just because that's what the group is doing, be the one who doesn't! Be unique! Be bold! Have confidence in your convictions! Hold fast to your beliefs! Some friends will come and go, but strengthening your friendship with Jesus will never disappoint you. Let Him show you how much He cares about you, especially in your loneliness when standing up for what is right. That's when His presence often seems the closest.

Dear Lord, I want to do what is right in Your eyes, no matter how lonely that feels sometimes. Please remind me that You are my constant and best friend. Amen.

ALWAYS THERE

If I go up to heaven, you are there; if I go down to the grave, you are there. If I ride the wings of the morning, if I dwell by the farthest oceans, even there your hand will guide me, and your strength will support me.

PSALM 139:8–10 NLT

Jodi and Lilly love when I tell stories about college days. They think it's fun to hear about my times going to class, eating in a big cafeteria, and living in a dorm with lots of friends and fun times and, of course, some major challenges along the way, too.

I graduated from Cedarville University, and my years there were truly some of the very best of my life. At times it was also some of the loneliest during my first couple of months when I didn't know many people and adjusting to a whole new life was really hard. But I look back now and remember how God pulled me closer to Him in those lonely times, and now I'm so thankful for them! He taught me so much about how I am actually never alone at all. His Holy Spirit is with me and knows my every thought and emotion and need. Sometimes it's truly a blessing not to have anyone to hang out with or any fun event to go to—if you focus on the fact that God is with you and always wants to hang out with you, and if you spend the time with Him!

Dear God, remind me that You are my very best friend and know me better than anyone else and that You're always available to hang out! Amen.

THINK ABOUT GOOD, NOT GARBAGE

Whatever is true, whatever is noble, whatever is right, whatever is pure, whatever is lovely, whatever is admirable—if anything is excellent or praiseworthy—think about such things.

PHILIPPIANS 4:8 NIV

I remember in high school joining some of my friends in watching popular horror movies and reading some scary books and going to haunted houses. Now I wish I hadn't. I wish I had followed the wisdom in this verse: "Don't copy the behavior and customs of this world, but let God transform you into a new person by changing the way you think. Then you will learn to know God's will for you, which is good and pleasing and perfect" (Romans 12:2 NLT). Years later, I still remember some of the awful scenes that can't seem to escape my brain. I don't care who calls me a big chicken—I'm now a big NON-fan of scary movies or haunted, gory houses and such. I believe it's very unwise to fill our minds with dark and evil things "just for the fun of it," even if they are just pretend. The Bible tells us, "When a good person gives in to the wicked, it's like dumping garbage in a stream of clear water" (Proverbs 25:26 CEV). I don't know about you, but I want my mind to be clear and free from garbage!

Dear God, please give me wisdom and good judgment to keep my mind free from evil things. Amen.

OUT OF DARKNESS, INTO LIGHT

He called you out of the darkness into his wonderful light.

1 Peter 2:9 NLT

Since we live in a world that gets darker every day with sin, it's important to let the light that is in us because of Jesus Christ shine so brightly that others might turn from darkness and come to know Him, too. We need to show others that we are different from the dark world around us. Ephesians 4:17–24 (CEV) states it with some pretty strong words: "As a follower of the Lord, I order you to stop living like stupid, godless people. Their minds are in the dark, and they are stubborn and ignorant and have missed out on the life that comes from God. They no longer have any feelings about what is right, and they are so greedy that they do all kinds of indecent things. But that isn't what you were taught about Jesus Christ. He is the truth, and you heard about him and learned about him. You were told that your foolish desires will destroy you and that you must give up your old way of life with all its bad habits. Let the Spirit change your way of thinking and make you into a new person. You were created to be like God, and so you must please him and be truly holy."

Dear God, please help me to turn from anything that is of the darkness and live in Your wonderful light. I know You only want what's best for me. Amen.

BY GRACE ALONE

We are made right with God by placing our faith in Jesus Christ. And this is true for everyone who believes, no matter who we are. For everyone has sinned; we all fall short of God's glorious standard. Yet God, in his grace, freely makes us right in his sight. He did this through Christ Jesus when he freed us from the penalty for our sins.

ROMANS 3:22–24 NLT

Some people believe it's the things you do and the way you follow rules that get you to heaven or a good eternal life. Not true! And how exhausting and stressful that would be! How could we ever do enough? Every major religion focuses on the deeds that must be done and the rules that must be followed to get to heaven—except true Christianity. Christianity focuses on what Jesus has already done and the fact that no one could ever possibly earn their way to heaven on their own. All that's required for a real relationship with God and for eternal life is faith in what Jesus has already done through His death and resurrection, and acceptance of His gift of grace. Ephesians 2:8–9 (NLT) says, "God saved you by his grace when you believed. And you can't take credit for this; it is a gift from God. Salvation is not a reward for the good things we have done, so none of us can boast about it."

Lord, I believe in You and I need You as my Savior from my sins. I'm so thankful for Your gift of grace, through faith alone, that has saved me. Amen.

BE LIKE A TREE!

"Just as you can identify a tree by its fruit, so you can identify people by their actions."
MATTHEW 7:20 NLT

When someone trusts Jesus as their Savior and has a true relationship with Him, they should be a bit like a good fruit tree. Just like a fruit tree is only healthy and growing correctly if it produces fruit, Christians are only healthy and growing correctly if they produce good fruit, too—meaning the good deeds they do in their lives, the way they care for others, and the actions and habits that clearly show they love and follow Jesus and live by His Word. The good things you do are not what gain you salvation, but you were created by God to do good things for Him. As you trust and follow Him, He brings you opportunities to do the good things He has planned. The Bible tells us in Ephesians 2:10 (NIV), "For we are God's handiwork, created in Christ Jesus to do good works, which God prepared in advance for us to do."

Dear God, show me the good things You have planned for me to do. There's nothing better I can do with my life. Amen.

ON YOUR BEST BEHAVIOR

Always let others see you behaving properly.
1 Peter 2:12 CEV

It's not your good deeds that get you to heaven, but with the right attitude—knowing that it's grace through faith alone that begins your relationship with Jesus Christ and gives you eternal life—following rules and laws and doing good deeds is the smartest way to live. In fact, the Bible talks about living such a good life that no one can ever accuse you of doing anything wrong: "Dear friends, you are foreigners and strangers on this earth. So I beg you not to surrender to those desires that fight against you. Always let others see you behaving properly, even though they may still accuse you of doing wrong. Then on the day of judgment, they will honor God by telling the good things they saw you do. The Lord wants you to obey all human authorities, especially the Emperor, who rules over everyone. You must also obey governors, because they are sent by the Emperor to punish criminals and to praise good citizens. God wants you to silence stupid and ignorant people by doing right. You are free, but still you are God's servants, and you must not use your freedom as an excuse for doing wrong. Respect everyone and show special love for God's people. Honor God and respect the Emperor" (1 Peter 2:11–17 CEV).

Dear God, please help me to have good behavior, because I want to honor You and point others to You. Amen.

NOTHING SEPARATES FROM GOD'S LOVE!

Nothing can ever separate us from God's love. Neither death nor life, neither angels nor demons, neither our fears for today nor our worries about tomorrow—not even the powers of hell can separate us from God's love. No power in the sky above or in the earth below—indeed, nothing in all creation will ever be able to separate us from the love of God that is revealed in Christ Jesus our Lord.

ROMANS 8:38–39 NLT

If you have specific fears either from things you imagine or from things that have happened to you, I encourage you to memorize the scripture above.

Of course, there are so many wonderful scriptures to memorize about God protecting us, so don't stop once you've memorized this one. Here are more to look up, read, and remember. God's Word is your best weapon to be brave in this world!

- Isaiah 41:10
- 1 Peter 5:7
- Psalm 56:3–4
- Ephesians 6:10–18
- Psalm 91
- Psalm 27

Heavenly Father, I trust that You are always near me, always providing for me, always protecting me, always loving me. Nothing can ever separate me from You, and because of that I have nothing to fear. Amen.

REAL BEAUTY

"People judge by outward appearance,
but the LORD looks at the heart."
1 SAMUEL 16:7 NLT

My heart hurts when I see countless magazine covers in stores that tell girls like you and women like me that beauty comes from the outside, from what our bodies and faces look like and what we wear. It's so not true! It's such a cruel lie that is pushed on you at pretty much every single turn in this world. Don't believe it, no matter how hard that is to do! There is nothing wrong with a nice outer appearance and clothes, of course, and a healthy body is certainly a good goal to honor our heavenly Father who gave us our bodies. But the appearance of your body never determines your worth and your real beauty. Your true beauty comes from the fact that you were created by God and made in His image. People look at the outward appearance, but God looks at your heart; and if you've accepted Jesus Christ as your Savior, then He sees you covered in His amazing grace and you are perfect in His sight.

God, help me to ignore the lies of the world that tell me that beauty means my reflection in the mirror has to match all the magazine covers. Help me to be confident that I am priceless and beautiful because You are awesome, and I am created by You! Amen.

Beauty from Within

Don't be concerned about the outward beauty of fancy hairstyles, expensive jewelry, or beautiful clothes. You should clothe yourselves instead with the beauty that comes from within, the unfading beauty of a gentle and quiet spirit, which is so precious to God.

1 Peter 3:3–4 NLT

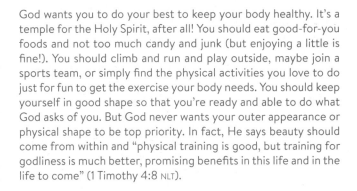

God wants you to do your best to keep your body healthy. It's a temple for the Holy Spirit, after all! You should eat good-for-you foods and not too much candy and junk (but enjoying a little is fine!). You should climb and run and play outside, maybe join a sports team, or simply find the physical activities you love to do just for fun to get the exercise your body needs. You should keep yourself in good shape so that you're ready and able to do what God asks of you. But God never wants your outer appearance or physical shape to be top priority. In fact, He says beauty should come from within and "physical training is good, but training for godliness is much better, promising benefits in this life and in the life to come" (1 Timothy 4:8 NLT).

Dear God, how I love and serve You comes first, because You look at my heart. Help me see my beauty like You do, from the inside out. Help me be spiritually healthy first of all and then physically fit. Amen.

STOPPING THE SCREAM

A person without self-control is like a city with broken-down walls.

Proverbs 25:28 NLT

Do you ever find yourself in a situation where you just want to SCREAM?!?! Sometimes it's so hard to hold it in! Without trying to gossip or complain about others, later you might just need to vent to someone you trust about the angry emotions you had and the way you wanted to act in response *but didn't*. That's the key, and that's what self-control is.

Our sinful nature gives us lots of emotions in response to situations and plenty of ideas of how to react that would not please God. What matters is what you do with those unhealthy responses. As hard as it is sometimes, you need to let them go and act according to God's Word—with patience, kindness, and love. That doesn't mean you always have to be a doormat, letting others walk all over you and never boldly stating your opinions or disagreeing. You can disagree and be firm but still be kind and compassionate. You never have to choose one of those over the other. You can disagree strongly with others and still be kind. You can practice self-control over your words and actions.

God, please help me to control my actions and reactions. Amen.

MESS INTO A MESSAGE

"Come now, let's settle this," says the LORD. "Though your sins are like scarlet, I will make them as white as snow."

ISAIAH 1:18 NLT

I don't like to clean up messes, yet I'm super good at making them! What's your favorite kind of mess to make? Or do you always keep things neat and tidy?

Messes make me think of the saying I've heard that "Only God can turn a mess into a message, a trial into a triumph, and a victim into a victory." What an encouraging reminder! Our lives might look kind of chaotic and untidy here on earth because we're constantly slopping through the major muck that sin causes in our own lives and the lives of everyone around us. But God is turning the messes into messages. Because of grace, He pulls us out of our sin and mistakes and helps us get back on track and work them out for good and His glory so that we can share our stories with others and help them see His grace, too. Praise Him for that! He's the only one who can take the ugliest, filthiest things and make them as white and clean as fresh new snow!

Dear Lord, I praise You for Your amazing grace You give time and time and time again! Thank You for turning messes into messages for others to know Your grace, too. Amen.

TRIAL INTO TRIUMPH

My friends, be glad, even if you have a lot of trouble.

James 1:2 CEV

Anyone who says the Christian life is easy and *only* full of blessing and prosperity is flat-out wrong. Jesus guarantees it Himself when He says in John 16:33 (NIV), "In this world you will have trouble. But take heart! I have overcome the world."

There are many more places in the Bible that talk about how to endure trials, too. For example, God uses trials to test us (1 Peter 4:12–13) and to strengthen us in our faith (James 1:2–4) and to develop our endurance, character, and hope (Romans 5:3–5)!

As the saying goes, "Only God can turn a mess into a message, *a trial into a triumph*, and a victim into a victory." Every trial will turn into triumph. Sometimes we'll see those triumphs in our lives here on earth, and some trials won't be fully resolved until heaven, but ultimately Jesus has triumphed over every kind of trouble because He has overcome the world!

Lord Jesus, please help me in all my troubles and those of my loved ones, too. Only You have the power to help us overcome them because You overcame the whole world! That is so cool, and I'm so thankful for You! Amen.

VICTIM INTO VICTORY

Joseph had a dream, and when he told his brothers about it, they hated him more than ever.

Genesis 37:5 NLT

If you have siblings, I sure hope your relationship with them isn't anything like Joseph in the Bible. His brothers were SO nasty to him—first they wanted to kill him, but then they had a little mercy and sold him into slavery instead. Yikes! Such meanies!

Joseph was definitely the victim of some incredibly cruel treatment. (Read the whole story in Genesis 37:1–50:26.) My favorite lesson from Joseph's account is how he was faithful to God even through *years* of waiting and hardship and betrayal. And instead of being bitter and cruel to his brothers in return when he had the perfect opportunity, he said to them, "Don't be afraid of me. Am I God, that I can punish you? You intended to harm me, but God intended it all for good. He brought me to this position so I could save the lives of many people. No, don't be afraid. I will continue to take care of you and your children" (Genesis 50:19–21 NLT).

If you are ever the victim of someone treating you cruelly, keep faith in God to help you. Remember Joseph's words: "You intended to harm me, but God intended it all for good." Keep following God, and He will turn your suffering into awesome victory!

Dear God, thank You for encouraging me with Joseph's story. I want to be a lot like him. Amen.

WHEN PEOPLE MOCK YOU

So be strong and courageous!
DEUTERONOMY 31:6 NLT

One night I was sitting in a café, and I overheard a group of teenagers saying nasty things about a classmate of theirs who was a Christian. I prayed for him, and I prayed for his mockers as well. And very soon, the Holy Spirit brought this scripture to my mind: " 'God blesses you when people mock you and persecute you and lie about you and say all sorts of evil things against you because you are my followers. Be happy about it! Be very glad! For a great reward awaits you in heaven' " (Matthew 5:11–12 NLT).

It's really hard to think of it as a blessing to get made fun of. But the Bible tells us to celebrate it! God hears each instance, He's keeping track, and He rewards loyalty and love for Him. The fact that this group even knew to tease their classmate for being a Christian shows that he wasn't hiding his faith, and God is pleased by that! If you're ever made fun of because you follow Jesus, remember this scripture. God knows and blesses every moment that you ever suffer for Him.

Dear Lord, help me to keep the right perspective if I'm made fun of for following You. I trust that You care and will bless me. Amen.

WILLING TO WAIT

Wait for the Lord; be strong,
and let your heart take courage; wait for the Lord!
Psalm 27:14 ESV

I used to be in 4-H when I was younger, and maybe you are now! I worked on dog obedience with my beautiful collie named Lad. I love dogs! It's so amazing to watch a well-trained pup! Even just the command to "Wait" when they see a yummy treat but are not allowed to get it right away is so cool! They want it so badly, but they're obedient to a good master because they know the reward of pleasing him or her is better than just the instant pleasure of getting the treat immediately.

Sometimes I need to take lessons from furry friends who are trained well. I don't always like to wait on God. Too often, I want to get things done or have what I need according to my own time frame, not someone else's. I find myself wishing all the time that He would hurry up already, both with answering prayer requests and just coming back again to make all things right in the world. But the Bible says that with God a day is like a thousand years, and a thousand years are like a day (2 Peter 3:8). I don't fully understand His ways or His timeline, but I trust that He is my good Master and I want to obey Him well, even while I'm waiting.

Dear God, when I need to wait, please help me
do it with a good attitude and with faith in You! Amen.

LISTEN AND DO

But don't just listen to God's word. You must do what it says. Otherwise, you are only fooling yourselves. For if you listen to the word and don't obey, it is like glancing at your face in a mirror. You see yourself, walk away, and forget what you look like. But if you look carefully into the perfect law that sets you free, and if you do what it says and don't forget what you heard, then God will bless you for doing it.

JAMES 1:22–25 NLT

Our family enjoys watching cooking shows on Netflix, but none of us are awesome cooks. We just don't often use what we learn from the shows in our kitchen. We seem to stick to the same old simple recipes we've been using for years. Hopefully that will change and we'll start applying what we learn by trying some new recipes. . . .

We could watch a zillion more hours of cooking shows on TV, and if we keep on just watching and never doing any of the things we see, then what good is it other than a bit of entertainment?

The Bible should never be thought of as some simple storybook for entertainment. It is living and active and sharper than any two-edged sword (Hebrews 4:12). It's our guide for life, and we cannot treat it like a cooking show we only watch for fun.

Dear God, I don't want to just listen to Your Word; I want to do it. I want to live out my faith for Your glory. Amen.

CHOOSING GOOD FRIENDS

"Bad company corrupts good character."
1 Corinthians 15:33 nlt

We love to eat apples, and there are so many yummy varieties—many with fun names. Pink Lady is a new favorite of ours. Ginger Gold and Gala and Golden Delicious are also top on our list of faves. We gobble them up, but sometimes when we stock up on a bunch at once, we have to be careful not to let one rotting spot on one apple spoil several more around or soon they're all bad!

Maybe you've heard the saying that "One bad apple spoils the whole barrel." Have you ever thought of that in regard to the types of friends you make?

The Bible says, "Bad company corrupts good character," or as another version puts it, "Bad friends will destroy you" (cev). You can think about it like that one rotten apple ruining the ones around it. If one friend in a group enjoys doing disobedient and dangerous things and is constantly encouraging the rest of the group to do likewise, then the whole group can easily turn bad. Be careful, then, when choosing your friends and joining groups of friends. Bad can so easily rub off on you because peer pressure is so strong at your age. Resist bad company, run away from it, and then wait and watch how God rewards.

Dear God, please help me avoid bad company among my friends and peers. I know it will only lead me to trouble to hang out with people who enjoy doing bad things. Help me be strong against peer pressure. Amen.

NO FUN

Why am I discouraged? Why is my heart so sad?
I will put my hope in God! I will praise him
again—my Savior and my God!
Psalm 43:5 NLT

I don't know why the word *fun* is in the word *funk*, because a funk certainly isn't any fun. Do you ever feel like you're walking around with a gloomy gray rain cloud hovering just over your head—or worse, one that's black with an angry thunderstorm? Sometimes you can't even really explain why you feel depressed or angry, you just do. Or maybe your personal or family or school situations seem just too hard to deal with.

Let God shoo away the funky clouds and lift your spirit. He does not always take all the troubles or reasons for your funk away, but He will walk with you right through them. You can focus your eyes and your attitude on hoping in Him, trusting that He will work all things together for good (Romans 8:28).

Dear God, when I'm down in a funk,
please lift me up. My hope is in You. Amen.

COMFORT OTHERS

God is our merciful Father and the source of all comfort.
He comforts us in all our troubles so that we can comfort
others. When they are troubled, we will be able to
give them the same comfort God has given us.

2 Corinthians 1:3–4 NLT

Our big dog Jasper is just about the cuddliest and nicest dog you could ever meet. (He even plays dress-up with us but is also a protective watchdog.) I wish I could let everyone in the world have some snuggle time with him when they're feeling sad. He's so soft and sweet to pet, and there's something so comforting about having him near when you're feeling sad.

The Bible tells us that God is the source of all comfort (I think good pets are part of His way of providing us comfort), and He comforts us so that we can comfort others. The more we need comfort, the more God gives, and the more we have to share with other people. And hopefully those people will want to know Jesus as their Savior because they've been shown much love in their hard times. God is working for good in every hard situation.

Dear God, thank You for being near and comforting me
in hard times. And thank You for pets that help comfort us, too.
Please help me share all the comfort You give with
others and point them to You. Amen.

SO MUCH MORE

Now to him who is able to do immeasurably more than all we ask or imagine, according to his power that is at work within us, to him be glory in the church and in Christ Jesus throughout all generations, for ever and ever!

Ephesians 3:20–21 NIV

Do you like to give long and specific wish lists, you know, just so everyone has a good idea of what you'd like for Christmas and birthdays? ☺ God wants to hear your wish lists, too. We can absolutely pray specifically about our needs, worries, fears, and even dreams and goals and things we want! As long as we are constantly asking with humility, knowing that God is sovereign and good over all things, and we are praying ultimately for God's will, God wants to hear about everything in our prayers, even the most specific. He wants us to depend on Him and trust Him. He wants a constant conversation with us. Remember, though, that it would be foolish to expect or even hope that God would answer every prayer exactly like we wish would happen. Why? Because He is able to do IMMEASURABLY more than anything we can dream up! There have been some amazing times in my life when I can look back and see when I prayed for something, was so SURE it was the very best thing, was so disappointed when it didn't work out, and then God did something SO much better than what I had asked to answer that prayer. I'm so glad God doesn't always do what I ask!

God, thank You for listening to all my prayers and requests. But thank You for not always answering them the way I want. Your ways and Your blessings are so much better than I can ever dream of! Amen.

ENDLESS GRACE

In fact, I don't understand why I act the way I do.
I don't do what I know is right. I do the things I hate.
ROMANS 7:15 CEV

Sometimes I feel absolutely sure that God just might give up on me today, that I've messed up one too many times and now He won't forgive me. I wonder why on earth I keep messing up in the same ways over and over. My struggles especially come from not guarding the words I say as carefully as I should. But I quickly have to remember that thinking God won't forgive me is a total lie! God's grace is endless, and He forgives again and again and takes our sins as far as the east is from the west (Psalm 103:12). Oh, how thankful I am for that!

I'm encouraged by the fact that there was no perfect person other than Jesus in the Bible. God loves and saves and uses regular sinners just like you and me! David who was called a man after God's own heart had some seriously shady moments, and Paul who wrote so much of the New Testament was once a murderer of Christians. Yet God loved and saved and used them both for good. He turned them from their sins, just like He turns us from ours. Be sad for your sin (2 Corinthians 7:10) and let the sadness lead you to repentance (which means to ask for forgiveness), but then don't hold it against yourself anymore. God doesn't, so why on earth should you?!

Dear God, I need Your amazing grace so much! Thank You so much for forgiving my sin again and again and again. I can't even describe how grateful I am. Amen.

WHERE GOD LEADS

We can make our plans,
but the Lord *determines our steps.*
Proverbs 16:9 NLT

Have you ever planned for something and then nothing went according to your plan? Sometimes what you expect to happen is so different from reality. Lilly remembers a particular birthday party for a friend where she had a plan in her mind of how things would go, but then the real party was nothing like what she had hoped for and expected. Still, she needed to make the best of it and focus on what was going right at the party (cupcakes, for one! Yum!) and the blessing of just being there. There are so many times in life when you will make a plan, but something will happen to change it. God is sovereign over everything, and He determines our actual steps. Make your plans, but know that ultimately your path will follow exactly where He leads.

Dear God, I just want to follow You because I know You lead me in exactly the right way. Help me to make wise plans but hold them loosely, knowing that You allow and direct changes to them according to Your perfect will! Amen.

GUARD AGAINST GREED

"A person is a fool to store up earthly wealth but not have a rich relationship with God."

Luke 12:21 NLT

Do you keep any collections like Shopkins, Beanie Boos, Num Noms, or Tsum Tsums? They're all adorable and so much fun! I admit I love them almost as much as Jodi and Lilly do! The Beanie Boos especially! I like to tease that their big glittery eyes are hypnotic and they make you want to buy them just by staring into them. "I'm so cute and sparkly! Take me home and love me," they seem to repeat over and over! But they just keep coming out with more cute characters and collections and extra-special, ultra-rare ones! Yikes, it's so hard to keep up!

It's fun to have toys and collections, as long as you don't get carried away. Remember to be thankful for what you already have, not just greedy for more. Jesus told the parable of the rich fool in Luke 12:15–21 and said, "Beware! Guard against every kind of greed. Life is not measured by how much you own" (v. 15 NLT).

Dear God, thank You for my many blessings! I know it's okay to play and enjoy things, just please give me wisdom about them, and help me not to be greedy. Amen.

UNIQUELY BEAUTIFUL

So God created man in his own image, in the image of God he created him; male and female he created them.

GENESIS 1:27 ESV

Maybe you enjoy playing with Barbies or maybe you don't, but I think it's pretty cool that they're making the dolls in a better variety of shapes and sizes. Even if the new dolls don't get it exactly right, they're at least helping more people appreciate that *all* girls are beautifully unique in height, weight, skin color, hair, and features.

No one else is exactly like you! Don't let the world get you down if you don't fit into a cookie-cutter idea of what's stylish and gorgeous. Be yourself and be comfortable; do your best to keep your body healthy; consider what the Bible says about modesty and how Christians should represent themselves in the clothing they wear; and then don't stress what the world says looks good or doesn't. The Bible says, "Charm can be deceiving, and beauty fades away, but a woman who honors the LORD deserves to be praised" (Proverbs 31:30 CEV).

I know this is a tough one that pretty much every girl struggles with in our world, but every day when you look in the mirror, try praying this scripture to God: "I praise you because I am fearfully and wonderfully made; your works are wonderful, I know that full well" (Psalm 139:14 NIV).

Dear God, I want to praise You more for how I am wonderfully made and not compare myself to the world's standard of beauty. Please help me to look in the mirror on both good days and bad with confidence because I am created beautifully in Your image and I am loved by You! Amen.

DEALING WITH THE DIFFICULT

Don't be hateful to people, just because they are hateful to you. Rather, be good to each other and to everyone else.

1 THESSALONIANS 5:15 CEV

I'm sure you already know how hard it can be to deal with difficult people. It's sad to say, but you're going to have to deal with a lot of them in your life—in school, in activities, in your church, and in all sorts of ways later on in your life as a grown-up, too. Many difficult people will make you want to give up and quit the area of your life that involves them, or they'll push you toward conflict.

The first thing to think about, though, is how you can often be a difficult person yourself and how you need so much grace; so ask God to help you give the same kind of grace that He constantly gives you. Then you have to pray for wisdom for God to show you if you need to get out of a situation, or if He wants you to stay in it and He'll help see you through it. And then you listen and wait for His answers, which are often so much better than you ever expected. God wants you to do your best to live at peace with everyone (Romans 12:18), and He will help you deal with difficult people in wise ways if you wait patiently for Him to show you.

Dear Lord, please help me to deal kindly and peacefully with people in my life who are so difficult to be around. Amen.

BE A LITTLE CLUELESS

For the wisdom of this world is foolishness in God's sight.
1 CORINTHIANS 3:19 NIV

Have you ever been in a group of friends or classmates and you don't have a clue what everyone else is talking about because it's something you're not allowed to do or watch or read? I remember so well how terrible that feeling is. It can make you feel left out and like you want to sink through the floor with embarrassment—but only if you let it!

I know it's so hard to deal with the peer pressure to fit in and not get teased. I remember and totally get it. But I promise you, as you get older, it will get so much easier. If you stay confident in whose you are (God's!), whom He made you to be, and how He wants you to live, and *don't* go along with the crowd just so that you don't feel clueless, you will reach a point where you look back and wonder why it EVER mattered.

The Bible says the wisdom of this world is foolishness in God's sight (1 Corinthians 3:19). That doesn't mean you shouldn't learn anything here on earth and you get to quit school. Nice try! ☺ But it does mean that it's totally okay to be a little clueless (or even a lot!) to the sinful things of this world. Satan is looking for all kinds of ways to destroy you. Pressuring you to go along with the harmful things that others are doing so that you don't feel left out is one of his favorite tricks—but you can fight back if you know that being clued in to God's Word and following it is far, far better than being clued in to the crowd.

Dear God, help me be clueless to the harmful things of this world but totally clued in to You! Amen.

GET OUT OF LINE!

Don't copy the behavior and customs of this world, but let God transform you into a new person by changing the way you think. Then you will learn to know God's will for you, which is good and pleasing and perfect.

ROMANS 12:2 NLT

It seems so silly how our culture tells you to be unique and be yourself but then often pressures you into things just because everyone else is doing it. Sometimes that's no big deal, and sometimes it's extremely harmful. On an episode of *Brain Games* recently, Jodi learned and laughed about how many people do things just because they see others doing them, even when they have no idea why. One example was people forming a line in a city. . .so many people just joined right in without any clue what they were waiting for. How ridiculous, right? Not a big deal if it's for a free doughnut or something, but what if everyone's lining up to watch a movie you know is not good for you? Or to gossip about a classmate and plan a mean trick on her? In those cases, GET OUT OF LINE!

No friend should ever force you to go along with anything that makes you feel uncomfortable—that uncomfortable feeling could very well be because the Holy Spirit is whispering to you to stop and waving red flags of warning. And He's saying follow Me and My ways in the Bible instead.

Dear God, help me be smart to never even join the lines of people doing sinful things; but if I happen to get into one, please give me the wisdom to quickly get out! Amen.

NOT ASHAMED!

For I am not ashamed of this Good News about Christ.
It is the power of God at work, saving everyone who believes.
ROMANS 1:16 NLT

Christianity is made fun of in so many ways and places in popular culture these days. TV shows, movies, books, and music love to make fun of being a Christian. That can be so discouraging, but it makes me focus on the fact that the devil is doing everything he can to keep people from believing in Jesus—and the devil has no reason to make others want to ridicule Jesus if Jesus is not the one and only hope of salvation. So, the more people are opposing and making fun of Christianity, the more it shows that Jesus absolutely is the Way, the Truth, and the Life and that no one gets to God except through Him (John 14:6)! He truly lived and died and rose again to save you from your sins. That's the Good News, and there's nothing to make fun of about that amazing hope we have!

So when you encounter people laughing at Christianity, don't let it get you down or embarrassed or ashamed, and in fact let it strengthen your faith! Keep on loving people, sharing the Good News, and believing and following God's Word anyway—and say like Paul did: "I am not ashamed of this Good News about Christ. It is the power of God at work, saving everyone who believes" (Romans 1:16 NLT).

Dear God, please help me to not let the ridicule of You
by this world ever let me lose faith in You! Amen.

LITTLE SUPERHEROES

Don't let anyone think less of you because you are young. Be an example to all believers in what you say, in the way you live, in your love, your faith, and your purity.

1 Timothy 4:12 NLT

As the youngest of four kids, when I was little I sometimes felt like the least important one in the family. All my older siblings seemed to be doing much cooler things than I was allowed to do, and sometimes it felt like anything I was doing didn't really matter or everyone else had been there, done that.

But by staying close to God, He helped me see the blessing in 1 Timothy 4:12. And He helped me focus on the good plans He had for *me*. God has a unique story for everyone individually, and if we constantly try to compare or see if we're doing better or more important things than those around us, we lose our focus on pleasing God with what He's given us to do.

No matter your age or where you are in your lineup of siblings or if you're an only child or what anyone tells you about your worth, believe that you absolutely matter to God. You can be His little superhero when you believe in His plans for you and depend on His supernatural power.

Dear God, I know I matter to You, and that's what matters most about me! Help me to do Your will for my life. Amen.

LET GOD LIFT YOU

How great is God's love for all who worship him?
Greater than the distance between heaven and earth!
How far has the Lord *taken our sins from us?*
Farther than the distance from east to west!

Psalm 103:11–12 cev

If you're ever feeling down because you've messed up and you just can't get things right, you need to follow the cure in this scripture and let God lift you up: "So humble yourselves before God. Resist the devil, and he will flee from you. Come close to God, and God will come close to you. Wash your hands, you sinners; purify your hearts, for your loyalty is divided between God and the world. Let there be tears for what you have done. Let there be sorrow and deep grief. Let there be sadness instead of laughter, and gloom instead of joy. Humble yourselves before the Lord, and he will lift you up in honor" (James 4:7–10 nlt).

Yes, be sad for a time over your mistakes. Admit them and ask for forgiveness from God and from any people you need to. And then when you have washed your hands and purified your heart of the sin because of God's grace, you can be confident that God has taken your sin away as far as the east is from the west. Praise and thank Him for that! He's so good and loves you so much. He wants to cover you with grace and lift you up in honor!

Dear God, I'm so sorry and sad about my sin. Please help me to turn completely away from it and from my enemy. Please help me to ask forgiveness from others when I need to, too. I need Your grace to cover my mistakes. I praise and thank You that it does! I ask You to lift me up! Amen.

FRIENDS FOREVER

A friend loves at all times.
PROVERBS 17:17 ESV

If you ever need help on how to be a good friend, the Bible is the best source of advice for BFFs!

Here are some scriptures to read and put into practice with your friends now and as you make more friends throughout your whole life!

> *"Do to others as you would have them do to you."* LUKE 6:31 NIV

> *God loves you and has chosen you as his own special people. So be gentle, kind, humble, meek, and patient. Put up with each other, and forgive anyone who does you wrong, just as Christ has forgiven you. Love is more important than anything else. It is what ties everything completely together.* COLOSSIANS 3:12–14 CEV

> *My friends, you are spiritual. So if someone is trapped in sin, you should gently lead that person back to the right path. But watch out, and don't be tempted yourself. You obey the law of Christ when you offer each other a helping hand.* GALATIANS 6:1–2 CEV

> *Don't use foul or abusive language. Let everything you say be good and helpful, so that your words will be an encouragement to those who hear them.* EPHESIANS 4:29 NLT

Dear God, please help me to have good friends and be a good friend. Amen.

WORKING HARD, DOING YOUR BEST

Whatever you do, do it all for the glory of God.
1 Corinthians 10:31 niv

In school, it's easy to get distracted by what your classmates are doing. It's fun to chat and be silly, and there are times for that, but you know those things can get you in trouble if you're supposed to be working. Galatians 6:4–5 (nlt) says, "Pay careful attention to your own work, for then you will get the satisfaction of a job well done, and you won't need to compare yourself to anyone else. For we are each responsible for our own conduct."

Whether or not you find it hard to focus on your schoolwork sometimes, let God's Word inspire you to always do your best on it, not just to please your teacher or your parents but to worship God through it! Work hard and do your best for His glory! Praising and worshipping God is never just singing songs and saying nice things to and about Him. Those are great, too, of course, but worship is so much of what we do and how we work with the abilities He has given us.

Dear God, please help me to focus on my work when I need to and focus on You at the same time! I want my work to make You happy and bring You praise because I'm doing my best with what You've given me! Amen.

WITHOUT GRUMBLING

Do everything without grumbling or arguing.
PHILIPPIANS 2:14 NIV

Think about your most hated chore or schoolwork assignment. It stinks, right? I have plenty of household chores and tasks that aren't my favorite, either. But time and time again when I have a bad attitude about them, I realize how much worse I make them, and they usually take me longer to do! And the times I'm smart and turn on some music or focus on blessings instead of complaining or, best yet, talk to God while I'm doing the task, everything goes so much better and faster, too! Time flies when you're having fun, right? Try to make the tasks you hate fun in some way, or at least be positive about them if you just can't think of them as fun. ☺

The Bible says that in everything we do or say, we have the opportunity to represent Jesus in it! "And let the peace that comes from Christ rule in your hearts. For as members of one body you are called to live in peace. And always be thankful. Let the message about Christ, in all its richness, fill your lives. Teach and counsel each other with all the wisdom he gives. Sing psalms and hymns and spiritual songs to God with thankful hearts. And whatever you do or say, do it as a representative of the Lord Jesus, giving thanks through him to God the Father" (Colossians 3:15–17 NLT).

Dear Lord, remind me that grumbling just makes everything worse. When I'm doing a task I don't enjoy, please help me to remember that I represent You in everything I do and that I need to keep a good attitude and a grateful heart. Amen.

STOP WORRYING

You will keep in perfect peace all who trust in you,
all whose thoughts are fixed on you!
ISAIAH 26:3 NLT

Have you ever gotten a nasty sunburn and then put that cooling aloe gel on? Ahhhh, sweet relief! That's how I feel about this scripture every time I repeat it when I'm feeling anxious. I've lain awake at night, and have spent all day sometimes, too, focusing on this scripture. I pray it to God while I also pray that He helps me keep my focus on Him during times when everything feels so out of my control. He is our amazing, endless source of real peace! His Word says, "Don't worry about anything; instead, pray about everything. Tell God what you need, and thank him for all he has done. Then you will experience God's peace, which exceeds anything we can understand. His peace will guard your hearts and minds as you live in Christ Jesus" (Philippians 4:6–7 NLT).

Whether you're worried about a big test at school tomorrow or the health of a loved one or other major problems in your family's, your friend's, or your own life, tell God *all* of them and let Him give you peace that He knows, He cares, He's good, and He's working for your good in all things.

Dear God, sometimes things in my life seem so out of control and I'm filled with such anxious thoughts. Please help me to keep my thoughts fixed on You. Fill my mind with Your goodness and truth from Your Word, and give me unexplainable peace. Thank You! Amen.

SUPPLYING YOUR NEEDS

And this same God who takes care of me
will supply all your needs from his glorious riches,
which have been given to us in Christ Jesus.

PHILIPPIANS 4:19 NLT

Maybe you have specific worries about your family having enough money for food, clothes, and shelter. If you do, read and remember Matthew 6:25–33 (NLT) where Jesus says: "That is why I tell you not to worry about everyday life—whether you have enough food and drink, or enough clothes to wear. Isn't life more than food, and your body more than clothing? Look at the birds. They don't plant or harvest or store food in barns, for your heavenly Father feeds them. And aren't you far more valuable to him than they are? Can all your worries add a single moment to your life? And why worry about your clothing? Look at the lilies of the field and how they grow. They don't work or make their clothing, yet Solomon in all his glory was not dressed as beautifully as they are. And if God cares so wonderfully for wildflowers that are here today and thrown into the fire tomorrow, he will certainly care for you. Why do you have so little faith? So don't worry about these things, saying, 'What will we eat? What will we drink? What will we wear?' These things dominate the thoughts of unbelievers, but your heavenly Father already knows all your needs. Seek the Kingdom of God above all else, and live righteously, and he will give you everything you need."

Dear God, help me to focus on following You and
then trust that You'll always give me everything I need.
You've promised that, and I believe You. Amen.

DON'T PLAY FAVORITES

For God does not show favoritism.
ROMANS 2:11 NLT

Do you still have a very favorite stuffed animal or blanket that you always, always, *always* have to sleep with at night? I took a very favorite blanket that I couldn't sleep without *to college* with me, so I completely understand!

Sometimes showing favoritism is totally okay. Sometimes it's totally not, like when treating some people better than other people. James 2:1–4 (CEV) talks about it: "My friends, if you have faith in our glorious Lord Jesus Christ, you won't treat some people better than others. Suppose a rich person wearing fancy clothes and a gold ring comes to one of your meetings. And suppose a poor person dressed in worn-out clothes also comes. You must not give the best seat to the one in fancy clothes and tell the one who is poor to stand at the side or sit on the floor. That is the same as saying that some people are better than others, and you would be acting like a crooked judge."

In God's eyes, every single person is created equal and every single person is equally valuable. Acts 10:34–36 (NLT) says, "Peter replied, 'I see very clearly that God shows no favoritism. In every nation he accepts those who fear him and do what is right. This is the message of Good News for the people of Israel—that there is peace with God through Jesus Christ, who is Lord of all.' "

Dear God, please help me to never treat any person better than any other. Amen.

UNFAILING LOVE

Praise the Lord! He is good. God's love never fails.
Praise the God of all gods. God's love never fails.
Praise the Lord of lords. God's love never fails.

Psalm 136:1–3 CEV

One time when Lilly was about three or so, she told me, "I don't like it when Jodi gets in trouble. I love her!"

I told her that was sweet, but I also said to her (because she was in a tattling phase at that time), "Why do you tattle on her sometimes just to get her in trouble?"

Lilly tearfully replied, "Sometimes I forget my love."

What an honest answer from a tiny little girl, one that everyone can relate to! I know I forget my love for others sometimes when I let angry or frustrated or stressed-out emotions take over. I'm guessing you do, too. We *all* do! Thankfully, we have God's grace to cover our mistakes and help us remember our love, ask for forgiveness, and restore the relationship. Thankfully, too, there is one source of love in our lives that is never forgotten and never leaves us—God's great love for us.

God's Word promises that "the steadfast love of the Lord never ceases; his mercies never come to an end; they are new every morning; great is your faithfulness" (Lamentations 3:22–23 ESV).

Heavenly Father, thank You that even though my love for others fails sometimes, and so does theirs for me, Your love never, ever fails. You never forget Your love for me. Help me to be more like You! Amen.

EVEN WITH THE LITTLE THINGS

"You are a good and faithful servant. I left you in charge of only a little, but now I will put you in charge of much more. Come and share in my happiness!"

MATTHEW 25:21 CEV

Just the other day, Jodi, Lilly, and I were buying a few things at the drugstore (including some Kit-Kats, yum!), and when we checked out, I was a little confused by the total. I knew it couldn't be right, because I'd added up in my head an estimate of what the total should be, and it was at least five dollars off. But the cashier had bagged up our items already and was telling us to have a good day. . . . I admit, a big voice in my brain was saying, "No big deal, you get to save five bucks today! It's not your fault the cashier didn't do his job right." But with God's grace, I was able to stop that voice. I knew that the cashier had accidentally put an item in my bag without my paying for it, and even though it wasn't on purpose, since I knew it had happened it would be a form of stealing if I didn't say something about it. So I did say something, and the cashier thanked me for making it right, and I was able to leave the store knowing I had done the honest and right thing. A clear conscience is worth far, far more than the five dollars I could have kept in my wallet.

Dear God, please help me to be honest even in the smallest kinds of things. I know You see everything, and I want to please You. I believe You bless me when You see I'm trustworthy. Amen.

TRUST GOD'S TIMING

The LORD is a God of justice.
Blessed are all who wait for him!
ISAIAH 30:18 NIV

Sometimes doing the right thing feels like it's getting you nowhere and doing what's wrong seems to be getting some people you know all the good stuff. Maybe you've seen someone cheating at school and they never get caught and they keep getting good grades, but you're studying hard and refusing to cheat and you can't ever seem to get an A. I know it's so hard, but wait on God. Keep doing what you know is right. Stop comparing your blessings with the people around you and let God deal with them if they are gaining things dishonestly.

Galatians 6:7–9 (NLT) says, "Don't be misled—you cannot mock the justice of God. You will always harvest what you plant. Those who live only to satisfy their own sinful nature will harvest decay and death from that sinful nature. But those who live to please the Spirit will harvest everlasting life from the Spirit. So let's not get tired of doing what is good. At just the right time we will reap a harvest of blessing if we don't give up."

Remember that it says, "at just the right time" your blessings will come. Let God see that you trust His timing and will keep doing good no matter what!

Dear Lord, I need help waiting on You when I'm trying to do the right thing but I feel like it's getting me nowhere. Help me to trust that You see and know and bless me when I'm trying my best to live for You. Amen.

TONGUE TAMING

Indeed, we all make many mistakes. For if we could control our tongues, we would be perfect and could also control ourselves in every other way.

James 3:2 NLT

You know how you blow a BIG bubble-gum bubble (so fun!) and within an instant it pops and you chew it all back into your mouth? Sometimes I wish the things I said were like that bubble. God's Word talks about how powerful our tongues are and how hard it can be to control them. I'm thankful He knows what a struggle it is. Our emotions seem to overtake our tongues too quickly sometimes, and before we know it, mean words are hanging out there in the air for others to hear and be hurt by—and we can't chew them back in like a popped bubble-gum bubble.

No, you can never get back the unkind or discouraging words you've said, but you can trust that God's grace covers them when you're sorry for them. Apologize to the person who was the target of your mean words and ask for forgiveness, knowing that everybody struggles with this! Then ask God for supernatural help in making your tongue obey His way.

Dear Lord, I pray like Psalm 141:3 that You take control of what I say and guard my lips. Please and thank You! Amen.

NO TROUBLE LASTS FOREVER

When his people pray for help, he listens and rescues them from their troubles. The LORD *is there to rescue all who are discouraged and have given up hope. The* LORD*'s people may suffer a lot, but he will always bring them safely through.*

PSALM 34:17–19 CEV

Think back to your worst *Alexander and the Terrible, Horrible, No Good, Very Bad Day* kind of day. We all have different stories of those kinds of days. Sadly, the older you get, the more kinds of bad days you have. But the more opportunity for all kinds of new *great* days, too!

On the bad days, no matter what kind, remember this encouraging scripture from 2 Corinthians 4:17–18 (NLT): "For our present troubles are small and won't last very long. Yet they produce for us a glory that vastly outweighs them and will last forever! So we don't look at the troubles we can see now; rather, we fix our gaze on things that cannot be seen. For the things we see now will soon be gone, but the things we cannot see will last forever."

Dear God, I need to remember that no trouble lasts forever, but eternal life and blessing with You does! Right now, You see me and hear me and know what I need in the midst of these troubles. Help me to trust You more. Amen.

STAYING OUT OF THE TRASH

Let us think of ways to motivate one another to acts of love and good works.
HEBREWS 10:24 NLT

Our dog Jasper is really good about staying out of the trash can—unless he's alone in the house and something smells really good to him in the trash can (so gross, right?). He's also good about never stealing food off the counter. . .unless we walk away and leave him alone near some kind of food lying out unwrapped. He gets overcome with temptation, and he just can't fight it when no one is around to help him remember the rules! He's tall when he stands on his hind legs, and one time I caught him when he'd just eaten half a loaf of delicious cranberry bread that I'd baked fresh and was letting cool on the kitchen counter. Bad dog, Jasper! Bad! (Good thing he's so sweet and cuddly and good most of the time!)

We can take a lesson from Jasper, that we all need people around to help us when we're tempted to do the wrong things. That's called having accountability. Our friends and family who love God can help keep us accountable to living according to His Word and doing our best not to sin when we're tempted.

Dear God, please surround me with people who love You and want to help me stay away from sin and on track with living well to please You. Amen.

DELIGHTING IN DIFFERENCES

Always be humble and gentle. Patiently put up with each other and love each other. Try your best to let God's Spirit keep your hearts united. Do this by living at peace.

EPHESIANS 4:2–3 CEV

Not long ago, we were on a road trip and stopped at an ice cream shop for some food and treats, and Jodi and Lilly got chocolate dipped ice cream bars. Lilly ate hers the "normal" way, but we laughed so hard when we saw that Jodi took off little tiny chunks of the coating with her fingers and soon had this hilarious-looking, naked ice cream bar.

Everyone does things a little differently, whether it's the way you eat your ice cram bar or the way you clean your room—and that's okay! We need to have patience with one another and give grace to one another, even when we sometimes wish others did things exactly the way we do. Sometimes we need to stop thinking that our way is *always* the best way of doing things. We can learn so much from others if we keep the right attitude of being humble and patient.

Dear God, help me to appreciate that You made everyone creative in their own ways. Remind me that I can learn so much from others when I'm humble, gentle, patient, and loving. Amen.

DUNKIN' DOUGHNUTS

When I am afraid, I put my trust in you.
Psalm 56:3 ESV

When Jodi and Lilly were younger, they did not want to learn to swim. Not at all. They loved being in the water, but they hated getting their faces wet. So, I made a silly swimming game called dunkin' doughnuts. Whoever was "it" had to think of a type of doughnut, and everyone else had to guess. If you didn't guess right, you had to dunk your face in the water.

Little by little and lots of games of dunkin' doughnuts and pool time later, the girls are now swimming just fine, and they realize how much they were missing out on by being afraid to get their faces wet. It's so fun to jump in the pool and swim underwater! Maybe learning to swim never bothered you, or maybe you can relate to this. Trying new things can be scary, but as long as you know it's a safe thing to do, you don't want to miss out on amazing fun by letting fear control you. Let God help you come up with ways to help you get over your fear. Think up silly games like we did, or ask a family member or friend to help you. Get creative and trust that when you're leaving your comfort zone, God is going with you. In fact, out of your comfort zone is often where God grows your faith in Him the most!

Dear God, help me to put my trust in You when I'm afraid of trying new things! I know You can make me brave. Amen.

FRUIT-OF-THE-SPIRIT PERKS

But the Holy Spirit produces this kind of fruit in our lives: love, joy, peace, patience, kindness, goodness, faithfulness, gentleness, and self-control.

GALATIANS 5:22–23 NLT

It seems like every store and business has some kind of perk card you can carry with you to earn points toward free stuff. I have so many cards filling my wallet it's hard to find the right one when I need it! I've noticed lately that in a world where so many people are impatient and rude over the slightest little thing, you often get a treat just for being patient and kind! Who even needs to carry those perk cards? For example, in just the past few months, the girls and I have gotten things like free ice cream, cookies, iced tea, and coffee at stores and restaurants just for using good manners and not being rude when we had to wait a little extra to be waited on or to pay. Because so many people don't use good manners anymore, employees of restaurants and stores are often majorly impressed by people who still use good manners.

Ask God to constantly grow the fruits of the Spirit in your life, and then watch and see how God blesses you when you use them with others. That's the very best kind of perk!

Dear God, please grow love, joy, peace, patience, kindness, goodness, faithfulness, gentleness, and self-control in me. Amen.

ALL THE LOVE

God is love.

1 John 4:16 NLT

I think Valentine's Day is so much fun. Pretty cards, hearts and flowers, and yummy candy! A celebration of love is wonderful, especially if you know the real source of love—God. The Bible says "we love because he first loved us" (1 John 4:19 NIV).

Our world has a lot of ideas about what real love is. Some are nice, but if they aren't inspired by God, then they aren't real love at all. The Bible says, "God is love, and all who live in love live in God, and God lives in them. And as we live in God, our love grows more perfect" (1 John 4:16–17 NLT). The only way to truly love one another is to keep walking with God and learning more about Him because He is love and the source of our love for others. Ask God to teach you more about real love each day and how to love others better with actions and not just words. First John 3:18–19 (NLT) says, "Dear children, let's not merely say that we love each other; let us show the truth by our actions. Our actions will show that we belong to the truth, so we will be confident when we stand before God."

Dear God, You are real love! Please help me to live in You and actively love others like You do. Amen.

ONE TRUE CREATOR

By faith we understand that the universe was created by the word of God, so that what is seen was not made out of things that are visible.
HEBREWS 11:3 ESV

These days it's far more popular to trust in science and Mother Nature than it is to believe there is one true God who is the Creator of our earth and the Creator of science itself. All the theories and formulas that scientists promote can make you doubt that God is for real. But simply look around at all the incredible plants and animals and humans! No scientist can explain how exactly they began growing and living and reproducing. Scientists have their theories, sure, but they don't have proof. How could anything begin here without a Creator creating it? Nothing else just appears that way. Everything that's made has to have a creator. Consider these powerful scriptures on creation, and praise our amazing God for His incredible handiwork!

> *"Worthy are you, our Lord and God, to receive glory and honor and power, for you created all things, and by your will they existed and were created."*
> REVELATION 4:11 ESV

> *In the beginning was the Word, and the Word was with God, and the Word was God. He was in the beginning with God. All things were made through him, and without him was not any thing made that was made.* JOHN 1:1–3 ESV

Dear God, I believe You are the one true Creator. Help my faith in You to grow each day, and show me more of You in Your creation. Amen.

MORE ABOUT CREATION

God saw all that he had made, and it was very good.

GENESIS 1:31 NIV

Here are more passages of scripture to encourage you to look at the world around you and believe that our God is a great and mighty Creator!

Job 12:7–10 (NIV) says, " 'But ask the animals, and they will teach you, or the birds in the sky, and they will tell you; or speak to the earth, and it will teach you, or let the fish in the sea inform you. Which of all these does not know that the hand of the LORD has done this? In his hand is the life of every creature and the breath of all mankind.' " I love this scripture because it reminds us that we humans are the ones with too many questions sometimes when clear answers are right there in front of us. The animals, even the fish and birds, know that God is our one true Creator! Studying all of earth's creatures should just give us more and more reason to trust and praise and learn more about God!

In Colossians 1:15–17 (CEV), we see again how Jesus is God Himself and also our Creator. He holds it all together! "Christ is exactly like God, who cannot be seen. He is the first-born Son, superior to all creation. Everything was created by him, everything in heaven and on earth, everything seen and unseen, including all forces and powers, and all rulers and authorities. All things were created by God's Son, and everything was made for him. God's Son was before all else, and by him everything is held together."

Dear Jesus, it boggles my mind to think about how You created all things, but I trust in You and I praise You for all of Your awesome work! Amen.

BELIEVING WITHOUT SEEING

For we live by believing and not by seeing.
2 Corinthians 5:7 NLT

Have you ever thought, *Sometimes I don't know if I believe Jesus is real or not because I can't see Him here*? At times it is really hard not to be able to see Jesus with our eyes and hear Him talk to us with our ears and touch Him and hug Him with our hands and arms. But Jesus said, "Have you believed because you have seen me? Blessed are those who have not seen and yet have believed" (John 20:29 ESV).

We don't have Jesus here with us right now, but we trust that He was here on earth in the past and that we do have the Holy Spirit with us now until Jesus comes back again. We can "see" the Holy Spirit, not with our eyes, but with our faith in Him and in the ways we sense Him leading us and talking to us, especially through the Bible.

And when we're struggling in our belief, we can pray like the man in Mark 9:24 (NLT) who said to Jesus, "I do believe, but help me overcome my unbelief!"

Dear Jesus, I'm sorry for the times that I doubt You are real. Remind me of the many ways You have shown me You are here through Your Holy Spirit. I trust You, and when my faith is weakening, please quickly strengthen it again. Amen.

ALWAYS WATCHING

Nothing in all creation is hidden from God. Everything is naked and exposed before his eyes, and he is the one to whom we are accountable.

HEBREWS 4:13 NLT

We laugh every time at the part in *Monsters, Inc.* when Roz says, "I'm watching you. . .always watching." A creepy monster/secretary is not always watching you, but God always is! With Jesus as your Savior, that never needs to freak you out, either. Even though you still make mistakes sometimes and God sees those, they are covered by the grace of Jesus if you've accepted Him. Since you know the Holy Spirit is always with you and God is always watching, let that inspire your best behavior. But when you mess up, remember that He's there and quickly ask for forgiveness—and ask Him to help you make things right again. He's such a good God who loves you more than anyone ever has or ever will, and He only wants what's best for you. You never have to be afraid of His constant presence in your life.

Dear God, I trust that You are with me and see and know everything I'm thinking and doing. Because of Your grace, that's not something to feel weird about, but to feel thankful for! Amen.

WINDING PATHS

How great is our Lord! His power is absolute!
His understanding is beyond comprehension!
Psalm 147:5 NLT

I didn't start geometry in school until the ninth grade, but it seems you kids are smarter these days and learning it much younger! So maybe you've already learned the geometry rule that the shortest distance between two points is a straight line. That rule always makes me think about how God definitely does not follow the ways of this world. Isaiah 55:8–9 (NLT) says, " 'My thoughts are nothing like your thoughts,' says the Lord. 'And my ways are far beyond anything you could imagine. For just as the heavens are higher than the earth, so my ways are higher than your ways and my thoughts higher than your thoughts.' "

I look back on my life and see how God has gotten me from point A to point B with a lot of curvy and sometimes complicated lines with lots of ups and downs. And there were often a lot of people on those paths whom I needed to meet and experiences I needed to grow through. And sometimes I stepped off the path God wanted for me and did my own thing and later needed to find my way back to God's way. Your life already likely hasn't been a series of perfect straight lines that go up and to the right; and if you're following closely to God, you'll see how He uses challenges and detours to draw you even closer to Him and to accomplish His will.

Dear God, keep me close, and help me to trust You
in all the winding paths of my life. Amen.

TIME TRAVEL

"Remember how the Lord your God led you through the wilderness for these forty years, humbling you and testing you to prove your character, and to find out whether or not you would obey his commands."

Deuteronomy 8:2 NLT

Time travel really would be amazing, right? It's fun to think about where you would go and whom you would visit in what time periods of the past. Do you know that if you're struggling with something and wondering how God is going to help, it's really smart to do a little time travel in your mind? Go back in your memories and think about all the ways He's helped you and provided for you in the past. Praise and thank Him for those times, and let them inspire you to have great faith that He will surely help and provide for you again! He says in Isaiah 46:9 (NLT), "Remember the things I have done in the past. For I alone am God! I am God, and there is none like me."

Dear God, when I'm discouraged or worried about the future, help me to travel back in time in my mind. You've been here all my life, helping me and providing for me, and because I see Your work in the past, I will trust You for the future. Amen.

WHAT OTHERS HAVE

It's healthy to be content, but envy can eat you up.

PROVERBS 14:30 CEV

If you have siblings, you know it can be so hard not to be jealous, over things that they have that you don't or their accomplishments and talents. But you're going to make yourself miserable if you let yourself be overcome by the green-eyed monster. (Did you know that expression came from the famous writer William Shakespeare?) Not only now with your siblings but with others your entire life, there will be people everywhere who have things you do not—and that's okay!

Be grateful for what you have, and celebrate what others have, too. Read and remember what James 3:13–16 (NLT) says: "If you are wise and understand God's ways, prove it by living an honorable life, doing good works with the humility that comes from wisdom. But if you are bitterly jealous and there is selfish ambition in your heart, don't cover up the truth with boasting and lying. For jealousy and selfishness are not God's kind of wisdom. Such things are earthly, unspiritual, and demonic. For wherever there is jealousy and selfish ambition, there you will find disorder and evil of every kind."

Dear God, please help me to get rid of any kind of jealousy in my heart. I want to be more thankful for what I have and celebrate with others what they have. Amen.

FIGHTING SELFISHNESS

Don't be selfish.
PHILIPPIANS 2:3 NLT

What's your earliest memory? It's strange how our brains work and we can't remember much of when we were babies. I guess we might just remember a bunch of crying and sleeping and smelly diapers anyway, right? We'd also probably recall how one of the very first things we had to learn was how to share. As soon as we started to roll and crawl, our parents had to be on our case not to take things from others and not to try to keep things from others.

Selfishness is just in us right from the start of our baby days. It's part of our sin nature, and we have to constantly fight the urge to keep everything to ourselves for our own gain and pleasure. It's hard, I know, but the way to keep it in perspective is to realize that the way to have plenty in life is to constantly give it away! Jesus said in Luke 6:38 (NLT), "Give, and you will receive. Your gift will return to you in full—pressed down, shaken together to make room for more, running over, and poured into your lap. The amount you give will determine the amount you get back."

Dear God, I sure need Your grace when it comes to my selfishness. Please help me to fight it and always be generous and willing to share. Amen.

STORING UP REAL TREASURE

Remind the rich to be generous
and share what they have.
1 Timothy 6:18 CEV

Think about your favorite toys, games, clothes, photos, and such! Think about how blessed you are! As much as you love your stuff (I love mine, too!), remember that you didn't bring any of it into the world with you, and you won't take any of it out. First Timothy 6:7–9 (CEV) says, "We didn't bring anything into this world, and we won't take anything with us when we leave. So we should be satisfied just to have food and clothes. People who want to be rich fall into all sorts of temptations and traps. They are caught by foolish and harmful desires that drag them down and destroy them."

So, enjoy your stuff, but be content with just what you need, and always be willing to share your blessings and live by God's Word. When you do, you're storing up treasures in heaven that do last forever! Our minds can't even imagine how great they will be! Matthew 6:19–20 (CEV) says, "Don't store up treasures on earth! Moths and rust can destroy them, and thieves can break in and steal them. Instead, store up your treasures in heaven, where moths and rust cannot destroy them, and thieves cannot break in and steal them."

Dear God, thank You for all the cool stuff I'm blessed with.
Please help me not to hold on to it too tightly, though.
I want to live according to Your Word and store
forever-treasures in heaven. Amen.

BUBBLE UP!

A joyful heart is good medicine.
PROVERBS 17:22 ESV

Every once in a while, and the more often the better, everyone needs a good belly laugh that makes you giggle so hard you have tears coming out of the corners of your eyes and your tummy hurts! God wants you to have joy and good, happy thoughts! Especially when they are about Him! It's always okay to laugh and have fun because you have joy bubbling up inside you when you know that the source of all real joy is God Himself. Because you know He is your hope and salvation for forever, you can always focus on that and feel happy, even if other things going on in your life are not so happy. First Peter 1:8–9 (NLT) says, "You love him even though you have never seen him. Though you do not see him now, you trust him; and you rejoice with a glorious, inexpressible joy. The reward for trusting him will be the salvation of your souls."

So don't ever stop having joy! Philippians 4:4 (NLT) says, "Always be full of joy in the Lord. I say it again—rejoice!" And no matter what's going on in your day, remember that "this is the day that the LORD has made; let us rejoice and be glad in it" (Psalm 118:24 ESV).

Dear God, please fill me with Your supernatural kind of joy, all the time! Amen.

GENTLE GIRL OF GRACE

Your gentleness made me great.
PSALM 18:35 ESV

When I was around your age, I had a cat that let me dress him up in baby clothes and put him in my doll stroller and push him around! How I loved that cat! Plus he would sit in the basket of my bike and ride as I pedaled lap after lap around our driveway.

Now, our dog, Jasper, lets Jodi, Lilly, and me dress him up in all kinds of costume clothes and hats. We have such good times taking funny pictures of him. Someday we might just have to make a calendar of all the hilarious photos.

People sometimes wonder how on earth we have a dog that is so patient and easygoing to let kids dress him up. Mainly it's about being gentle with him. He would never tolerate it if we treated him roughly while putting silly outfits on him!

Gentleness is important with our pets, and even more importantly, the Bible talks about gentleness toward people. Gentleness is a fruit of the Spirit (Galatians 5:22–23), and gentleness is necessary when telling others about our hope in Jesus and in having good relationships with others (Ephesians 4:2; 1 Peter 3:15; Proverbs 15:1). Ask God to help you be a gentle girl as He grows you in His grace.

Dear God, please help me be gentle the way Your Word teaches me to. Amen.

PATIENCE AND PRAISE INSTEAD OF POUTING

Praise the Lord. Praise God in his sanctuary; praise him in his mighty heavens. Praise him for his acts of power; praise him for his surpassing greatness.

Psalm 150:1–2 niv

I'm not so great at fixing very many things, but Jodi and Lilly's dad is. Their grandpa and papa are, too. But sometimes when something breaks or needs a repair, we have to wait until Daddy, Grandpa, or Papa is home from work and available to help fix what's broken.

It's hard when a favorite toy breaks or your bike tire is flat or whatever and you can't do the things you planned to do. Waiting for a problem to be solved is usually no fun at all. Whatever you do, though, don't pout and complain. That never helps anything or anybody, and it will often just get you into trouble for a bad attitude. The Bible says, "Do everything without grumbling" (Philippians 2:14 niv).

Instead, you can learn to praise God in the waiting times. Focus on the blessings that you do have. Praise God for how awesome He is and for all His goodness! Get creative in figuring out something good to do during the wait time. Show others that you can be pleasantly patient even when things aren't going your way. God often blesses that kind of attitude in a totally cool new way that you never even thought of!

Dear God, please help me to have a good attitude during problems while I have to wait on the solutions. I want to praise You and be patient while I wait. Amen.

NEVER FORGOTTEN

The Lord answered, "Could a mother forget a child who nurses at her breast? Could she fail to love an infant who came from her own body? Even if a mother could forget, I will never forget you."

Isaiah 49:15 CEV

It's an awful feeling to be forgotten or left out. When life is really hard because of what you're going through, you might wonder if God has forgotten you. But the Bible promises that never happens. God never leaves you and constantly loves you, even if you can't always understand what He's doing or why He's not answering prayer the way you want Him to.

Isaiah 49:15 is talking about how difficult it would be for a good mom to forget a baby who is depending on her for everything. But if even she forgot, God would still never, ever forget. His love for you is greater and better than anyone else's love for you by far—and He doesn't make any mistakes.

Dear God, I know that You never forget me. You know and care about every single thing going on in my life. I trust You to help me deal with it in a good way! Amen.

AMAZING HANDIWORK

When I look at your heavens, the work of your fingers,
the moon and the stars, which you have set in place,
what is man that you are mindful of him,
and the son of man that you care for him?

Psalm 8:3–4 ESV

Not long ago, our family got to see the moon rise up over the ocean on a clear night with a full moon. While we sat on the beach, we also saw a shooting star. Wow! What a fascinating and beautiful sight! It's mind-boggling to consider how God created such beauty in the night sky! We will have so many cool things to learn when we spend forever with Him in heaven!

As God grows you as His girl of grace, make it your habit to look at the world around you both day and night and to praise Him when you see such amazing, unexplainable things in nature. The world wants you to praise science and research, and while those things are great and much needed, always give credit to God for His amazing work! He is the reason we have science to study!

God, I praise You for all Your amazing creation in the skies.
Your handiwork is amazing and beautiful! Amen.

SUPERCOOL SCIENCE

"Worthy are you, our Lord and God, to receive glory and honor and power, for you created all things, and by your will they existed and were created."

REVELATION 4:11 ESV

It's incredible how scientists do experiments and study how things work and build and engineer machines and solve problems and cure diseases and injuries, and on and on! No doubt, science is super cool, and it's interesting how recently there's a great emphasis on encouraging more girls to be scientists, like with Goldieblox toys and TV shows like *SciGirls* and *Project MC²*. Maybe you have dreams of being a scientist when you're all grown up!

I wonder how much better our scientific progress for healing illnesses and creating new things to help people in this world would be if more scientists gave credit to the one true God as the Creator of all science? There are some amazing Christ following scientists doing great work today, but what do you think might happen if even more scientists respected God and studied His Word along with studying science in the world He created? What might He reveal to them, and what breakthroughs might there be? That's something to pray for and something to consider for your life, too, if you love science!

Dear God, I pray for more scientists to acknowledge You as the Creator of all science, and I ask You to work through them to help our world. Amen.

LOVING ENEMIES

"You have heard the law that says, 'Love your neighbor' and hate your enemy. But I say, love your enemies! Pray for those who persecute you! In that way, you will be acting as true children of your Father in heaven. For he gives his sunlight to both the evil and the good, and he sends rain on the just and the unjust alike."

MATTHEW 5:43–45 NLT

Wow, Matthew 5:43–45 is not a fun scripture to read, right? It sure doesn't make you feel good. Anyone who thinks the Bible only has warm and fuzzy things to say to keep us comfortable doesn't know much at all about the Bible. It's hard to think of anything more *un*comfortable than showing love to and praying for people who don't like us and who mistreat us. And yet that's exactly what Jesus tells us to do in this scripture.

Is there someone who is being mean to you? Someone who lies about you and turns other people against you? Whatever the situation is, get help from a grown-up to make sure you're safe in the situation, and also start praying like crazy for the person mistreating you. Ask God to show you exactly how He wants you to show love. Proverbs 25:21–22 (NLT) gives some advice, too: "If your enemies are hungry, give them food to eat. If they are thirsty, give them water to drink. You will heap burning coals of shame on their heads, and the LORD will reward you."

Dear God, it's way too hard on my own to love people who are mean to me. Please show me how and exactly what to do. I trust You! Amen.

SLOW DOWN

*But you, O Lord, are a God of compassion and mercy,
slow to get angry and filled with unfailing love and faithfulness.*
PSALM 86:15 NLT

In the movie *Inside Out*, it's hilarious when the character Anger takes over. Usually his hot temper creates some kind of funny situation we can all relate to. But that's just a fiction story, and in real life, anger is not often very good for us. Anger is not always bad, but the Bible talks about being very slow to get angry. God is not quick to get angry, and if He were we'd be in a lot of trouble! Imagine how upset He would constantly be with people and our many mistakes!

When you're in a situation that makes you mad, literally take a deep breath and count to ten or take a little walk or scream into your pillow for a minute. Ecclesiastes 7:9 (NLT) says, "Control your temper, for anger labels you a fool." And James 1:19–20 (NIV) says, "Everyone should be quick to listen, slow to speak and slow to become angry, because human anger does not produce the righteousness that God desires."

As you work to control anger, think about mistakes you have made and be grateful that God has been slow to anger with you. Pray and thank God, and then let Him help you be slow to anger with others.

*Dear God, it's really hard not to get too upset sometimes.
Please help me to be like You in slowing down
anger when I feel it rising up in me. Amen.*

LEARN GOD FIRST

Don't be impressed with your own wisdom.
Instead, fear the LORD and turn away from evil.
PROVERBS 3:7 NLT

I'm guessing you enjoy learning new things and telling others about what you've learned, even if you don't always love doing your schoolwork. But does Proverbs 3:7 mean a girl of grace gets a pass on ever doing lessons and homework and studying anything new? Sorry, but no! There's a healthy balance in fearing the Lord, which means respecting Him first and letting true knowledge and wisdom result from your relationship with Him.

The Bible says in Proverbs 9:10 (NLT), "Fear of the LORD is the foundation of wisdom. Knowledge of the Holy One results in good judgment." God is the very beginning of all wisdom and knowledge. Respecting Him first is the only way to really know anything at all. It makes perfect sense that the source of learning about the world around us is the One who created it all in the first place! So rather than just being proud of yourself for learning new things, be thankful for new knowledge and proud of God for giving you the ability to learn, and thankful for who He is and what He has done!

God, You are the source for knowing and understanding anything about our world because You created it all! I praise You and thank You! Please help me to grow in You first and gain my knowledge and wisdom from my relationship with You. Amen.

A HEALTHY VIEW OF YOURSELF

Don't think you are better than you really are.
Be honest in your evaluation of yourselves,
measuring yourselves by the faith God has given us.
Romans 12:3 NLT

I hope you have amazing goals and dreams for your future, and I hope you look in the mirror and love the precious girl you see there—*you*! You are amazing and matter so much to God, no matter what you do! Our world talks a lot about pride in your own accomplishments and being a great and successful person. But the Bible talks very differently about how to view yourself. God doesn't ever want you to think you are worthless. He thinks you are so valuable that He sent His Son to die to save you, so obviously your worth is priceless! But a healthy perspective is to realize that *real* and lasting self-worth comes from your identity in Christ and the purposes He has created you for.

In this world, yes, it's possible to live without Jesus as Lord of your life, but no one can ever be truly fulfilled that way. They can make it look good from the outside, of course, but they will always be hollow inside without Jesus Christ. Ultimately, this world will seem like the briefest blink of an eye compared to eternity, and your value and status for eternity is based 100 percent on Jesus.

Dear God, help me to see myself as You do and do the things You have planned for me. I know You love me and value me more than anyone else ever does, ever has, ever will! Thank You! Amen.

TREASURE TROVE

Fear God and obey his commands, for this is everyone's duty. God will judge us for everything we do, including every secret thing, whether good or bad.

Ecclesiastes 12:13–14 NLT

No matter what your dream job is for the future, God has already given you a job for every day of your life. It doesn't pay in dollars and cents here on earth, but it's building up a treasure trove of blessings waiting in heaven for you. And who doesn't want their own treasure trove, right?

Our job and purpose in life is the fear of (or respect for) God and obedience to His commandments. This is "everyone's duty," says Solomon in the book of Ecclesiastes. The Bible has the simple yet profound and perfect answer to all of life's questions—the *only* answer that can ever genuinely fulfill, if only people will believe it and test it! Yet so many people try *anything but* the Bible for answers; they keep trying and working—and coming up empty.

The only really satisfying job you can ever find is to do what your Creator intended specifically for you, to obey Him in what He has designed and prepared. Ephesians 2:10 (NIV) says, "For we are God's handiwork, created in Christ Jesus to do good works, which God prepared in advance for us to do."

Dear God, please help me to respect You and Your commandments and to obey them. I need Your good guidance to show me all the good things You have planned for me to do! Amen.

OBEY AND BE BLESSED

"If you are willing and obedient, you will eat the good things of the land."
Isaiah 1:19 NIV

The Bible promises that obedience equals blessings. That sounds like a great math equation! Think about the verse above and also these:

> *Blessed are those who fear the Lord, who find great delight in his commands. Their children will be mighty in the land; the generation of the upright will be blessed. Wealth and riches are in their houses, and their righteousness endures forever.* Psalm 112:1–3 NIV

> *When the Lord takes pleasure in anyone's way, he causes their enemies to make peace with them.* Proverbs 16:7 NIV

The thing is, sometimes the world's idea of blessings confuses believers. Obeying God does not mean total riches and fun and constant good health and always happy times here on earth. It certainly can mean those things, but ultimately it means all these things and more in your *eternal* awesome home that God is creating.

It also means God's guidance and peace for any hard thing here in this sinful world as you obey His commands, no matter the circumstances or temptations to ignore them. Obedience to God means His constant, loving presence in your life. There is no better success and blessing than that!

Dear God, please help me to obey You the best I can in all situations. I know that is the best way to live to gain the best kind of blessings! Amen.

REAL-DEAL SERVANT OF GOD

For God is working in you, giving you the desire and the power to do what pleases him.

Philippians 2:13 NLT

Have you ever had a classmate in school who acts perfectly obedient and sweet in front of the teacher, but whenever Teacher turns away or it's time for recess, this classmate is mean and breaks every rule but just sneakily keeps out of trouble?

God doesn't want the kind of obedience that is just for show or for selfish rewards. He wants obedience that comes from a willing heart—a heart that loves Him and His Word and wants to produce the good fruit He has planned for those who follow Him. He wants obedience that is looking to please Him alone, no matter what people around you think or say.

A question to ask yourself regularly as God grows you to be a girl of grace is the one Paul asks in Galatians: "Am I now trying to win the approval of human beings, or of God? Or am I trying to please people? If I were still trying to please people, I would not be a servant of Christ" (Galatians 1:10 NIV).

Be a real-deal servant of Christ first of all, and then let Him help you serve others as He directs.

Dear God, I want to please You above all, no matter what. I want to be a real-deal servant of You! Amen.

FAMILY FEUDS

A wise woman builds her home, but a foolish woman tears it down with her own hands.

Proverbs 14:1 NLT

No one ever fights in our house. Ha! Just kidding. We absolutely fight and yell and stomp and slam doors sometimes. We're not proud of that, but we all know that families have their stressful times. Family feuds are impossible to avoid. The people you're related to and spend the most time with are bound to get on your nerves, and you'll drive them crazy sometimes, too! It's just part of being a family. But with God's grace, family members can always work through the conflicts and never give up on one another. First Timothy 5:8 (NLT) makes it clear that Christian families are meant to take care of one another when it says, "But those who won't care for their relatives, especially those in their own household, have denied the true faith. Such people are worse than unbelievers."

Sure it can be hard, but Romans 12 offers some good advice for keeping peace and keeping families together: "Be happy with those who are happy, and weep with those who weep. Live in harmony with each other. Don't be too proud to enjoy the company of ordinary people. And don't think you know it all! Never pay back evil with more evil. Do things in such a way that everyone can see you are honorable. Do all that you can to live in peace with everyone" (vv. 15–18 NLT).

Dear God, please help me to work out conflicts among family members quickly. I know You want us to take good care of one another. Amen.

FOR YOUR OWN GOOD

Praise the Lord*! Blessed is the man who fears the* Lord*,*
who greatly delights in his commandments!

Psalm 112:1 esv

Obedience and *discipline* are probably not words that make you want to do a happy dance, but a girl of grace knows that when done right, they are for her own good. We first learn to obey our parents, and then we learn that ultimately we are to obey God. And God is not a killjoy just trying to ruin all the fun! The commands He wants us to obey are never just to rain on our parades and stop our joy. He longs for us to obey Him so that He can protect us from sin in the world plus let us receive many blessings. First John 5:3 (esv) says, "For this is the love of God, that we keep his commandments. And his commandments are not burdensome."

And we need discipline to get us back on track when we don't obey, so that we'll remember why we need to obey in the first place. Proverbs 3:11–12 (nlt) says, "My child, don't reject the Lord's discipline, and don't be upset when he corrects you. For the Lord corrects those he loves, just as a father corrects a child in whom he delights."

Dear God, please help me to obey You in all things and
to appreciate discipline when I need it. I know that
You love me and just want what is best for me. Amen.

BE CHILDISH

When Jesus saw what was happening, he was angry with his disciples. He said to them, "Let the children come to me. Don't stop them! For the Kingdom of God belongs to those who are like these children."

Mark 10:14 NLT

Maybe you don't like being called a child because it makes you feel immature. Or you just can't wait to be a grown-up and make your own decisions. Of course growing in wisdom and maturity is a good thing, but don't ever let people make you feel bad or useless for being young. A real sign of maturity is being confident in the age you are and the abilities you have that come with that age. Trying to act older than your actual age totally backfires because those who are mature can recognize that kind of behavior as a sure sign of immaturity.

Consider what the Bible says about kids and being young. In Mark 10:14, Jesus was unhappy with the disciples for keeping kids away from him and said the kingdom of God belongs to those who have faith like children. Also, Matthew 18:10 (NLT) says, " 'Beware that you don't look down on any of these little ones. For I tell you that in heaven their angels are always in the presence of my heavenly Father.' " And 1 Timothy 4:12 (NLT) says, "Don't let anyone think less of you because you are young. Be an example to all believers in what you say, in the way you live, in your love, your faith, and your purity."

Dear God, You love children and young people and want to grow us and bless us in Your wisdom and love. Thank You! Amen.

GIVE AND TAKE

And he said, "Naked I came from my mother's womb, and naked shall I return. The Lord gave, and the Lord has taken away; blessed be the name of the Lord."

Job 1:21 ESV

I love the contemporary worship song called "Blessed Be Your Name." It's based on Job 1:21.

You've likely heard the story about Job. What a roller coaster his life was of blessings and then total loss and despair and finally blessings again. Through it all, he was faithful to God. Job had no "entitlement" problems like we hear of people having today. Some people these days feel like they're guaranteed certain blessings and opportunities in life. But Job knew that every person comes into the world with absolutely nothing, with no guarantees of what this life will be like, and with no way to take anything from this world into eternity. God alone is all-powerful, and He gives and takes away. We can choose to ignore or be angry with Him, or we can lean in close to Him and get to know Him better through His Word and His Spirit and praise Him through the times of both blessing and loss.

As God grows you to be a girl of grace, you will experience both good times and hard times. Choose to praise God in all things, no matter how difficult that might be, and then patiently wait while He changes you and makes His plans to bless you unimaginably for eternity.

Dear God, even when life is hard,
I want to praise Your name! Amen.

KNOWING GOD'S WILL

Always be joyful. Never stop praying. Be thankful in all circumstances, for this is God's will for you who belong to Christ Jesus.

1 Thessalonians 5:16–18 NLT

"I'm just not sure what God's will is." Maybe you've heard other Christians say this, and maybe you've said it yourself. Well, 1 Thessalonians 5:16–18 tells you what God's will is in every kind of situation. He wants you to have joy. He wants you to keep praying. He wants you to be thankful. Sounds simple, right? Well, sure, unless your situation is a really tough one—and who can avoid tough situations? We all struggle with all kinds of things, with all kinds of heartache and difficulty—and in those awful situations 1 Thessalonians 5:16–18 is sure a lot easier said than done.

Like anything you want to be great at, doing God's will takes practice. Again and again you must choose joy in your bad situation, remembering that real joy is not based on your circumstances but on the fact that God is with you and loves you. Choose to keep praying about every single thing, no matter how big or small, because the Bible says to cast ALL your anxiety on Him. And choose to give thanks for each of your blessings, listing them out in your conversations with God.

Dear God, help me to remember that Your Word shows me Your will for me in all things. Help me to constantly have joy, talk to You, and give You thanks. Amen.

WIDE, HIGH, LONG, DEEP

And may you have the power to understand, as all God's people should, how wide, how long, how high, and how deep his love is. May you experience the love of Christ, though it is too great to understand fully. Then you will be made complete with all the fullness of life and power that comes from God.

Ephesians 3:18–19 NLT

Do you ever have days when you just don't feel very lovable? Days when you feel sure that God just might give up on you because you keep making the same kinds of mistakes over and over? I do. It's on those days that Ephesians 3:18–19 is so encouraging to me, and I hope it is for you, too. In it, the author Paul, inspired by God, is praying for believers to realize how wide, long, high, and deep God's love is for us. It's a love that is far too great to understand fully, but that doesn't mean we shouldn't try! God wants us to keep talking to Him and spending time hearing from Him in His Word to better understand His love every single day.

God's love reaches so much farther than any distance or measure we can imagine, even past our doubts that make us wonder if there is a time that God might finally get fed up and stop loving us—never! He will *never* do that. God loves you unconditionally, even on the days you feel most unlovable!

Dear God, help me, each and every day, to understand more about Your great love for me. I'm so grateful for Your endless love! Amen.

WILLING TO WORK

Work willingly at whatever you do, as though you were working for the Lord rather than for people.
COLOSSIANS 3:23 NLT

One of my favorite memories of fifth grade is that I got to work in the school cafeteria. It was considered a privilege and a reward to get asked to work there. And it was so much fun, plus we earned a free lunch that day. We left class a little early, and the teacher trusted that we'd make up any work that we missed. We got to help serve food or put silverware on each tray, and when everyone was done, we sometimes helped wash trays. My favorite task was scooping corn, and something about our school cafeteria corn was so much better than any corn I've ever tasted elsewhere!

Our world is changing quite a bit. Too many people seem to be forgetting that the ability to work is a good thing, a blessing! Did you know that every little thing you do, even if it's just scooping out corn onto a cafeteria tray, can be a way to worship God? It is when you do it with a good attitude, as if God is your boss—because He is! He's the best boss ever, too, who loves and wants to bless you like no other.

Dear God, help me to remember that the ability to work is a blessing and that every act of work I do can be a form of praise to You! Amen.

PICK UP!

"Call to me and I will answer you."
JEREMIAH 33:3 ESV

Have you ever really wanted to talk to a particular person, but their phone just kept ringing and they didn't pick up? When Jodi and Lilly spent the night at their grandparents' recently, they tried to call me to say good night, but I didn't realize my phone was turned off, and we were all sad that we didn't get the chance to say good night to one another.

It's frustrating when we can't get through to someone we're trying to communicate with. Thankfully, we never have to beg God to "pick up!" and hear our requests. Through the Holy Spirit, God is listening to us all the time, every moment! God's Word encourages us to "pray in the Spirit at all times and on every occasion. Stay alert and be persistent in your prayers for all believers everywhere" (Ephesians 6:18 NLT). And even when we're not sure what to pray, that's totally okay because "the Holy Spirit helps us in our weakness. For example, we don't know what God wants us to pray for. But the Holy Spirit prays for us with groanings that cannot be expressed in words" (Romans 8:26 NLT).

Dear Lord, remind me that You constantly hear me, You constantly want me to tell You my thoughts, and You constantly want to help with my needs and the needs of others. Thank You! Amen.

POWERFUL AND EFFECTIVE

The prayer of a righteous person is powerful and effective.
JAMES 5:16 NIV

You never have to read this verse and think, *Well, I'm not good enough and I don't have the best behavior all the time, so there's no way my prayer is powerful and effective.* If you have asked Jesus Christ to remove your sin and be your Savior, then you are a righteous person. Anyone who has accepted Jesus has become perfect in God's sight, because Jesus paid the cost for our sin when He died on the cross.

So keep in mind every single time you pray that you are doing something powerful and effective like the Bible promises! Believe it! Then make a habit of constantly praying to God about all things, and watch what God does in your life and the lives of those you're praying for!

These verses on prayer will help motivate you to trust in the power of prayer more, too:

> *The righteous cry out, and the LORD hears them; he delivers them from all their troubles.* PSALM 34:17 NIV

> *And we are confident that he hears us whenever we ask for anything that pleases him. And since we know he hears us when we make our requests, we also know that he will give us what we ask for.* 1 JOHN 5:14–15 NLT

Dear God, please remind me all the time how much You want to hear from me in prayer. Help me to trust how powerful and effective prayer is! Amen.

WISDOM, NOT WAVES

Blessed is the one who finds wisdom,
and the one who gets understanding.
PROVERBS 3:13 ESV

We think boogie boarding on calm waves is super fun, but bouncing around endlessly on really rough waves? Probably not so much. It must be so scary (and nauseating!) to be completely unsteady and tossed by wind and rough waters. God doesn't want your life to be like a turbulent ride on rough waves, either. You just need to ask God for His wisdom, trust that He gives it generously, and then believe in it! He is ready and willing to make your journey through life steady and sure. That doesn't mean you won't ever have hard times, but your life will always be anchored in Him, giving you stability even when everything in the world around you is chaotic and scary. James 1:5–8 (NLT) says, "If you need wisdom, ask our generous God, and he will give it to you. He will not rebuke you for asking. But when you ask him, be sure that your faith is in God alone. Do not waver, for a person with divided loyalty is as unsettled as a wave of the sea that is blown and tossed by the wind. Such people should not expect to receive anything from the Lord. Their loyalty is divided between God and the world, and they are unstable in everything they do."

Dear God, I need Your wisdom in all things. I know You give it generously. I want to be loyal to You! Please give me more wisdom each day, and keep me stable in You. Amen.

THE RIGHT KIND OF LOVE

God is love.

1 John 4:8 ESV

God is love, and He wants those of us who love and serve Him to share Him with others so they will want a relationship with Him, too.

First Corinthians 13 is a popular passage to teach us about love. Read it again, and read it regularly to help you know how important love is and how to share it with the people God has placed in your life: "What if I could speak all languages of humans and of angels? If I did not love others, I would be nothing more than a noisy gong or a clanging cymbal. What if I could prophesy and understand all secrets and all knowledge? And what if I had faith that moved mountains? I would be nothing, unless I loved others. What if I gave away all that I owned and let myself be burned alive? I would gain nothing, unless I loved others. Love is kind and patient, never jealous, boastful, proud, or rude. Love isn't selfish or quick tempered. It doesn't keep a record of wrongs that others do. Love rejoices in the truth, but not in evil. Love is always supportive, loyal, hopeful, and trusting. Love never fails!" (vv. 1–8 CEV).

Dear God, help me to read and remember this scripture regularly and try my best to love others like You love. Amen.

MEMORY WORK

Everything in the Scriptures is God's Word. All of it is useful for teaching and helping people and for correcting them and showing them how to live. The Scriptures train God's servants to do all kinds of good deeds.

2 Timothy 3:16–17 cev

I hope you like to memorize Bible verses. It's a practice that's so incredibly valuable for your faith and relationship with God—and for sharing your hope in Jesus with others, too. I spent several years in middle school and high school on a Bible Quiz team and learned bunches of scripture. I've been amazed through my adult life how those verses pop into my mind just when I need them. I often don't even remember that I had memorized them until all of a sudden there they are in my brain! It's so cool how God works that way to bring truth from His Word to mind exactly at the right moment.

Psalm 119:10–11 (niv) says, "I seek you with all my heart; do not let me stray from your commands. I have hidden your word in my heart that I might not sin against you." That's another reason to memorize scripture and hide it in your heart—it helps to keep you from sinning against God. Remembering His truth and His commands helps you avoid bad choices.

If you don't already, start now writing down scriptures and posting them in places where you'll be reminded of them and practice them. Hide God's Word in your heart, and then see how He uses it in your life! You will not be disappointed!

Dear God, I want to study and memorize Your Word to help me live my life the best way possible and to share Your truth with others. Amen.

RESURRECTION

"He isn't here! He is risen from the dead!"
LUKE 24:6 NLT

At Easter time, I hope you get a basket full of chocolate and treats and maybe even get to hunt around for eggs. It's just so much fun to celebrate, especially when you know the real reason for any springtime holiday celebration is that Jesus died but ROSE AGAIN!

There are plenty of other religions that people follow in this world, but only Christianity is worth believing in because only Christianity worships and spreads the good news of a Savior who died but came back to life, with eyewitnesses to verify His resurrection.

His resurrection is what makes our faith have any purpose and strength. Even Paul said in 1 Corinthians 15, "Unless Christ was raised to life, your faith is useless. . . . If our hope in Christ is good only for this life, we are worse off than anyone else. But Christ has been raised to life! And he makes us certain that others will also be raised to life" (vv. 17, 19–20 CEV).

Your faith in Jesus is not useless because God raised Him from the dead, and your studying and following God's Word and keeping a relationship with God through Jesus is the best thing you can possibly do with your life! You are preparing here in this world for an awesome eternity in heaven!

Dear Jesus, I believe You rose from the dead, and I praise You! My salvation and faith in You are the very best things about my life. Amen.

WEIRD WATERSLIDE STORY

"This is my command—be strong and courageous! Do not be afraid or discouraged. For the LORD your God is with you wherever you go."

JOSHUA 1:9 NLT

I vividly remember a day when I was little and my family went to a water park in Branson, Missouri. I recall it so well because I was miserable. Miserable at a supercool water park. Weird, right?

I was miserable because I let my fear of trying something new control me. I desperately wanted to go down the big waterslides with my dad and three older siblings. But I just couldn't make myself do it. It seemed too scary. So all day, I pouted and cried until finally my mom picked me up and put me on my dad's lap just as he was about to start down the slide. There was no time for me to escape; we were suddenly flying down the slide. I screamed and cried and thought I'd never survive, and then just about the time we were at the bottom, I realized something: THIS WAS SO MUCH FUN!

I got out and wanted to go again and again, but guess what? The park was closing and we had to leave. Ugh, what a bummer! I'd wasted the whole day in fear over something I finally realized was incredibly fun.

Let the lesson I learned that day be a lesson to you, too. If wise grown-ups who love Jesus and whom you know you can trust are encouraging you to try something new, even if it seems scary, go ahead and try. Maybe you won't love it, but at least you'll know for sure. And maybe you will find something you love. To this day, I still love waterslides!

Dear God, help me to get over my fears that are keeping me from amazing things! Amen.

BE A STAR!

Do everything without grumbling or arguing, so that you may become blameless and pure, "children of God without fault in a warped and crooked generation." Then you will shine among them like stars in the sky as you hold firmly to the word of life.

PHILIPPIANS 2:14–16 NIV

In our world, being a star means being famous like a singer or actress or amazing athlete. But the Bible tells us we can shine like *real* stars in God's eyes by living a life that follows His Word and strives to be blameless and pure and without fault in a culture that loves to make sin look like so much fun. Such a huge part of that is doing what God asks of us without grumbling and arguing. That's sure easier said than done sometimes, right?

But if you keep in mind that what God asks of you is always what's best for you, it will help you to do things without fussing about them. Philippians 2:13 (NIV) says, "For it is God who works in you to will and to act in order to fulfill his good purpose." He doesn't expect you to do hard things without complaining about them all alone. He is with you, *in* you through His Holy Spirit helping you do them. So remember that and depend on Him. Then you're a real star!

Dear God, please help me to want to be the kind of star You want, not what the world says is a star. Amen.

THE BEST KIND OF REST

God gives rest to his loved ones.
PSALM 127:2 NLT

It's so hard for me to sleep at night without some noise. I've become addicted to just the sound of a fan blowing. (On cold nights I just point it against the wall so that it doesn't make me chillier!) The soothing, steady sound of it helps block out the normal creaks of the house or the wind outside—the kinds of noises that make me lie there and imagine creepy things.

Lots of people like what's called "white noise" to sleep, just a simple way to help get a good night's rest. Far more important for helping get good rest, though, is listening to what God's Word says about it. The best kind of rest comes from trusting in Him and living for Him!

> *If you are tired from carrying heavy burdens, come to me and I will give you rest. Take the yoke I give you. Put it on your shoulders and learn from me. I am gentle and humble, and you will find rest. This yoke is easy to bear, and this burden is light.*
> MATTHEW 11:28–30 CEV

> *In peace I will lie down and sleep, for you alone, O LORD, will keep me safe.* PSALM 4:8 NLT

Dear God, please help me to live a life that honors You and is full of good rest when I need it, the kind of rest that can only come from You! Amen.

NO LYING LIPS!

The Lord detests lying lips,
but he delights in those who tell the truth.
Proverbs 12:22 NLT

I have many fun babysitting stories, and some crazy ones, too—like the time when I was seventeen and I accidentally broke a coffee table with my rear end! I had just sat on the edge to reach down and pick up the baby off the floor to take him upstairs for his nap. But the center glass part of the table broke and I fell right through the middle of it! Yikes! I cut my hand, got a nasty painful scrape on my back, and had to quickly figure out how to vacuum up lots of glass before three very young kiddos got into it and hurt themselves.

After everyone was safe and everything cleaned up, I was so dreading telling the kids' mom! I admit it was tempting to make up a lie. I was embarrassed plus figured she might be mad plus worried that I'd have to use up most of the money I'd earned babysitting to buy them a new table. But I prayed and knew God wanted me to be honest. I admitted my embarrassing mistake and offered to buy the mom a new table. Thankfully, she was so kind and understanding and was just so grateful no one had been hurt worse.

Even if I'd had to pay for the table, I knew the best thing I could do in that situation was be honest. God always blesses honesty in one way or another or sometimes in a zillion ways!

Dear God, please help me to be honest even when it seems like making up a little lie would be so much easier. I know the truth in all things is so important. Amen.

ROAD TRIPS RULE!

Be still before the LORD and wait patiently for him.

PSALM 37:7 ESV

Our family loves to take road trips, especially to Florida! We have all flown before, too, and it's nice to get from one place to another in the speedy way that airplanes provide, but there's something so fun (and usually less expensive!) about a road trip. Enjoying the sights along the way, watching movies and reading books in the car, and stopping when you want to run around at a rest stop or eat a yummy meal at a restaurant we don't have in our home state of Ohio are some of our favorite things. Road trips also make you learn patience to get from one place to another, and that's a really good lesson for life.

God does not always get us from one point in our lives to where He wants us to be next in a quick and easy way. He often lets it take awhile, and we learn to patiently keep going, a little at a time, seeing and learning new things along the way, until we reach our next destination. He even lets hard and frustrating things happen, too—kind of like car trouble or a traffic jam on a road trip—to teach us more patience and to keep trusting that He will take care of us through hard times.

Dear God, help me to be more patient in life, not always wanting to get from one place to another in the quickest and easiest way. I know You often use waiting times to teach me new things and grow me more in Your grace. Amen.

LOVELY LIGHTS

Again Jesus spoke to them, saying, "I am the light of the world. Whoever follows me will not walk in darkness, but will have the light of life."

John 8:12 ESV

Have you ever been to a ginormous Christmas light display? Jodi, Lilly, and I love the ones that big zoos put on with what seems like a zillion twinkling colors! So many people in the world just think that the lights are pretty, but those of us who love Jesus know they are pretty *and* they remind us of the fact that Christmastime is when the Light of the World was born, Jesus! The Bible talks about how we have His light and can share it with others in our dark world. Read these scriptures, and work hard to shine your light on those around you!

> *For once you were full of darkness, but now you have light from the Lord. So live as people of light! For this light within you produces only what is good and right and true.* Ephesians 5:8–9 NLT

> *"You are the light of the world—like a city on a hilltop that cannot be hidden. No one lights a lamp and then puts it under a basket. Instead, a lamp is placed on a stand, where it gives light to everyone in the house. In the same way, let your good deeds shine out for all to see, so that everyone will praise your heavenly Father."* Matthew 5:14–16 NLT

Dear Jesus, help me shine brightly to share Your love! Amen.

YOUR VALUE

"What is the price of two sparrows—one copper coin? But not a single sparrow can fall to the ground without your Father knowing it. And the very hairs on your head are all numbered. So don't be afraid; you are more valuable to God than a whole flock of sparrows."

MATTHEW 10:29–31 NLT

I read a great little example on Facebook one time that talked about how when you buy a new tablet or smartphone, most people instantly buy both a protective cover for the screen and a case that provides protection, too. It seems sad, then, that so many girls these days, each of whom is FAR more valuable (especially in God's eyes) than any electronic device, don't value themselves enough to cover and protect themselves wisely with clothes. I don't mean girls have to only wear things that cover skin from head to toe or always have to be completely out of fashion. It's absolutely possible to both wear cute, fashionable clothes *and* protect and value and respect your body, knowing it's just a fact that sin in the world causes some people to look at girls' bodies with bad thoughts and plans.

While your body is not the most important thing about you (your soul that lives forever is!), it's so incredibly valuable because it carries your beautiful soul! Ask God to help you to be wise in respecting your body and protecting it from harm and from sin in smart ways, including the way you dress!

Dear God, the world gives me such confusing ideas on what's cool to wear. Please help me know how to value and respect and protect my body wisely. Amen.

DANCING FOR THE LORD

And David danced before the Lord with all his might.
2 Samuel 6:14 NLT

I have very little coordination or artistic physical ability, so I don't really ever dance unless it's just for silly fun, and it's probably ridiculous to watch—LOL! But I do enjoy watching dance, especially watching my girls, Jodi and Lilly! They're part of a church dance group that's not for competition but just for fun and recreation and to be an act of worship to God. Their instructors choose worship music to dance to, and it's such a beautiful sight to watch young people honor God with lovely movement to songs that praise Him with their words.

Our sinful world has turned a lot of dancing into something that does not please God. But when done in good ways, dancing makes God happy, and the Bible talks about it! Read these scriptures and ask God to help you dance with joy—whether it's in a class or on a competition dance team or just for fun wherever you are—in ways that praise Him and make Him smile!

> *Let them praise his name with dancing, making melody to him.* Psalm 149:3 ESV

> *Praise the Lord! Praise God in his sanctuary; praise him in his mighty heaven! Praise him for his mighty works; praise his unequaled greatness! Praise him with a blast of the ram's horn; praise him with the lyre and harp! Praise him with the tambourine and dancing.* Psalm 150:1–4 NLT

Dear God, when I dance I want it to be in ways that please You! You are awesome, and I praise You!! Amen.

SING A SONG!

Oh come, let us sing to the LORD*; let us make a joyful noise to the rock of our salvation! . . . Let us make a joyful noise to him with songs of praise!*

PSALM 95:1–2 ESV

It's amazing how many different styles of music there are and what talent people have for music! God gave people so much creativity when He created us. That makes sense, since we are created in His image and He is obviously so creative! ☺

I love how many different kinds of songs and lyrics there are now that praise God. If you fill your mind with scripture and praise for God through song, you are so smart! Do you know why? Because when hard times come, your mind will know where to focus and you will find yourself gaining so much strength from God! And even when you're not going through a hard time, you'll just constantly be filled with so much joy in worshipping God!

Read all these scriptures to help you know how important praising God through song is!

> *I will sing to the* LORD *because he is good to me.*
> PSALM 13:6 NLT

> *I will sing to the* LORD *as long as I live; I will sing praise to my God while I have being.* PSALM 104:33 ESV

> *Sing to him, sing praises to him; tell of all his wondrous works!* PSALM 105:2 ESV

Dear God, I want my mind and my mouth to be constantly full of praise to You! Please help me to choose music wisely. You are so worthy of praise! Amen.

THOSE EMBARRASSING MOMENTS

With all humility and gentleness, with patience, bearing with one another in love.

Ephesians 4:2 ESV

Do you like to tell embarrassing-moments stories with your friends? Sometimes it's more fun to hear them from others than tell our own because they're still embarrassing long after they happened! LOL! One time my best friend and roommate in college came back to our dorm room and told me a good one. She had been in biology lab class and all of a sudden got a little sleepy or something and fell off her stool! The worst part? No one else laughed with her. (We sure did laugh together when she told me, though! Hahaha!)

Sometimes it would feel better to have people laugh with us when something embarrassing happens than to just stare at us in shock, right? The Bible says there is "a time to weep, and a time to laugh" (Ecclesiastes 3:4 ESV). As long as others are not being cruel in their laughter and are helping out if the embarrassed person needs it, then finding the humor together in an embarrassing situation actually helps a lot! We all need to not take ourselves too seriously sometimes and remember that everyone makes silly mistakes and has embarrassing moments. Every. Single. One of us.

Dear God, please help me to have grace and good humor in embarrassing situations. Amen.

HEAVENLY HOME

For we know that when this earthly tent we live in is taken down (that is, when we die and leave this earthly body), we will have a house in heaven, an eternal body made for us by God himself and not by human hands.

2 Corinthians 5:1 NLT

Do you like to watch any of those home-improvement or house-hunting shows on TV? We do! Especially *Fixer Upper*. It's so fun to see how an old house in need of lots of repair gets an amazing makeover!

Better than any house design or makeover that we can imagine here on earth is the amazing home God is making for us in heaven! John 14:1–3 (NLT) says, " 'Don't let your hearts be troubled. Trust in God, and trust also in me. There is more than enough room in my Father's home. If this were not so, would I have told you that I am going to prepare a place for you? When everything is ready, I will come and get you, so that you will always be with me where I am.' "

It's fun to try to dream about all the amazing things God is getting ready for our forever home in heaven! I'm really hoping for some cool waterslides! What do you like to imagine will be there?

Dear God, You are amazing, and I know You must be making heaven beyond my wildest and coolest dreams! Help me to keep living according to Your Word and living with confident hope of my forever home with You. Amen.

LIFE'S NOT FAIR

But if you do what is wrong,
you will be paid back for the wrong you have done.
COLOSSIANS 3:25 NLT

It's not fair! How many times have you said or thought those words? I can't even begin to count in my own life! So many things in your life are not going to seem fair. It's best just to accept that frustrating fact while you're young. The world became dramatically unfair the moment sin entered in the garden of Eden. I know it's such a bummer, but don't let it discourage you.

God is watching you, helping you, and blessing you along the way—with just enough to keep you trusting in Him and His plans for you day by day. He's watching when you're doing the right thing but keep getting knocked down or overlooked while those who aren't following God's ways seem to keep getting ahead. (*Grrr*, right?) He will make sure those who do wrong get what they deserve, and He will make everything good and right for those who follow Him—if not right now, then for sure forever in heaven someday. Remember that the world is absolutely unfair, but God is absolutely not. Hebrews 6:10 (NLT) says, "For God is not unjust. He will not forget how hard you have worked for him and how you have shown your love to him by caring for other believers, as you still do."

Dear God, please help me to keep up my good work
living a life that honors You. I know You will
make all things fair someday. Amen.

OVERCOMERS!

Do not be overcome by evil, but overcome evil with good.
Romans 12:21 NIV

Romans 12:21 is a scripture I repeat again and again in my head when I hear bad news of yet another thing gone wrong in our world or when I experience something bad myself. It gives me motivation to keep on loving all the people around me and helping others in the best ways I can. A good habit to get into is to read this verse, memorize it, and apply it specifically when something is going wrong in your life or in the world and you want to do something to help. For example, you could think:

I will not be overcome by this classmate who is being mean to me. I can overcome her cruel actions with love and kindness and prayer for her.

Or

I should not be overcome by this hard family situation I'm in. I can overcome with hope and trust in God for my family and by being loving and helpful to my family.

Or

I will not be overcome by worry and fear over the bad things going on in our world. I can overcome by asking God how to show His love in my home and in my church and in my community.

Or all of the above! Now you think of some to apply to your own life!

Dear God, I know You can help me not to be overcome by all the bad stuff in this world. You are good, and I know You can help me to DO good toward others until You return and get rid of all evil. Amen.

SUPERGIRLS!

Faith makes us sure of what we hope for and gives us proof of what we cannot see. It was their faith that made our ancestors pleasing to God.

HEBREWS 11:1–2 CEV

Superheroes are kind of a big deal, right?! And they're not just for boys anymore. Maybe you love the movies like *Batman* and *Superman*, and maybe you've seen and even have some of the DC Superhero girl dolls and shows.

There's nothing wrong with enjoying superhero stories, as long as you keep the right perspective. Those are fiction, just for fun, but the Bible talks about the *real-deal* heroes—people strong in their faith in the one true God; people who truly had supernatural power because they believed in God, listened to God, and let God work in their lives!

One of the best places to read about many of them is in Hebrews chapter 11. You'll read snippets there about the great faith of Abel, Enoch, Noah, Abraham, Sarah, Isaac, Joseph, Moses, Rahab, Gideon, Barak, Samson, Jephthah, David, Samuel, and the prophets. Hopefully that will make you want to look up more details of their stories in the rest of the Bible.

You can believe in God, listen to God, and let God work in your life at all times, too! Then you truly will be a superhero, too—a Supergirl of Faith!

Dear God, please inspire me with the stories of real superheroes—people who believe wholeheartedly in You and in Your power. I want to be like them! By Your power and grace, please make me a Supergirl of Faith! Amen.

MORE SUPERGIRLS

God is within her, she will not fall.
Psalm 46:5 NIV

Spend some time in the stories of women in the Bible to inspire you as you grow to be a girl of grace. Ruth and Esther have whole books of the Old Testament dedicated to telling their stories of faith and courage and the way God worked through them.

Deborah was one of the judges of Israel who helped show God's loving care of His people. Her story is in Judges chapters 4 and 5.

Hannah's story in 1 Samuel 1 and 2 is of great faith, persistent prayer, and commitment to God.

And of course Mary the mother of Jesus, whose story is told especially in the Gospel of Luke, is quite the heroic girl who was trusted to carry the hope of the world and be the earthly mother to God in human form!

These are just a few of the courageous women in the Bible. The main thing to remember about their lives is that they were humble girls who loved God and had great faith in His power, not in their own abilities. A true Supergirl knows that the only kind of power that is real is God's power.

Dear God, I'm amazed by the women in the Bible whom You used for great things! Please help me to trust in Your power, and use me for great things, too! Amen.

HIDE-AND-SEEK

Anyone who wants to come to him must believe that God exists and that he rewards those who sincerely seek him.

HEBREWS 11:6 NLT

I'm guessing you've played a lot of games of hide-and-seek with your family and your friends! It's a classic! My favorite hiding spot is in a bathroom shower. Jodi's is in a closet. Lilly's is under a table. What's yours?

While hide-and-seek is fun, I'm glad that trying to find God is not a game where He's hoping not to be found! It's terribly sad when people today think God doesn't exist because they can't find Him or talk to Him exactly like they do a person here on earth. Or maybe they prayed to Him and didn't get the answers they wanted, so they don't think He's for real. Or maybe they think, sure, God has to exist but He doesn't care one bit what people do or what happens to them.

Those people aren't spending any quality time in God's Word. "For the word of God is alive and powerful," Hebrews 4:12 (NLT) says. And they aren't seeking God sincerely. He promises in Jeremiah 29:13 (NIV), "You will seek me and find me when you seek me with all your heart."

For all those who *do* truly look for God, they will find what a good Father He is, a Father who wants to have a loving, constant relationship with His children and guide them in the awesome plans He created them for (Ephesians 2:20; Jeremiah 29:11)!

Dear God, help me to always remember that You are never hard to find. Please keep me close to You through Your Spirit and Your Word, and help me to show others how to find You, too. Amen.

BIRTHDAY BLESSINGS

You are the one who put me together inside my mother's body, and I praise you because of the wonderful way you created me.
PSALM 139:13–14 CEV

We love to make a big deal about birthdays! It's a time to celebrate the wonderful people God has created. Birthdays are also a great time to remember the blessing prayers that are in the Bible. They're called *benedictions*, which is a fun word to say! A cool tradition for birthdays is to pray these benedictions over the one who is celebrating.

Have a loved one pray these for you on your next birthday, and you can pray them for others on their special days, too! It's an awesome way to celebrate a year of life that has passed and to bless the next year that is coming!

> *" 'May the LORD bless you and protect you. May the LORD smile on you and be gracious to you. May the LORD show you his favor and give you his peace.' "* NUMBERS 6:24–26 NLT

> *May the God of hope fill you with all joy and peace in believing, so that by the power of the Holy Spirit you may abound in hope.* ROMANS 15:13 ESV

> *I pray that God will make you ready to obey him and that you will always be eager to do right. May Jesus help you do what pleases God. To Jesus Christ be glory forever and ever! Amen.* HEBREWS 13:21 CEV

Dear God, thank You for the fun of birthdays, and thank You for the prayers of blessing in Your Word! Amen.

WEIRD IN THE WORLD

Dear friends, you are foreigners and strangers on this earth.
1 Peter 2:11 CEV

Do you ever feel a little embarrassed by your family when you're out in public? Maybe your mom has danced down the aisles of Wal-Mart just to be silly. (I'd never do that to Jodi and Lilly! Haha! Just kidding! Yes, I have!)

Guess what? You need to stop being worried about feeling embarrassed or weird in this world because the Bible tells you that you *should* feel weird in this world! True, it does not say anything specific about whether moms should dance down the aisles in Wal-Mart, but it does talk about living in the world as strangers in a foreign land (1 Peter 1:17; Hebrews 13:14). It also talks about how the world hates those who follow Jesus (Matthew 10:22). And it commands us not to conform to the ways of this world (Romans 12:2).

No one needs to be obnoxious and try to seem crazy and purposefully make others think Christians are to be avoided, and my dancing example is just for fun. The point is, as Christians we just have to realize that we never will really fit into the culture of this world and that's a *good* thing. God has better plans and ways and wants you to let Him "change the way you think. Then you will know how to do everything that is good and pleasing to him" (Romans 12:2 CEV).

Dear God, help me to not worry about feeling weird in this world. Please help me to focus on You and how You want me to live. Amen.

CRAZY BUTTERFLIES

I love you, LORD, my strength.

PSALM 18:1 NIV

Do you have something that really makes the butterflies flap around like crazy in your stomach? The thing that does it for me is speaking in front of big groups of people. One-on-one or in a small group, I love to chat, but talking in front of a big crowd? Not so much.

Psalm 18:1 is such an excellent and easy verse to memorize to help you when you're nervous about anything at all—piano or dance recitals, a big gymnastics meet, working on diving in swim class, a big test you have to take or speech you have to give at school. In just a few short words, this scripture focuses your thoughts on God and your love for Him, knowing He loves you, too, and reminds you that He is your strength to do anything.

Maybe you've heard this verse, too—"I can do everything through Christ, who gives me strength" (Philippians 4:13 NLT). It's another awesome scripture to memorize and repeat, time and time again, when you're faced with any kind of challenge that stirs up those butterflies!

Dear God, there are all kinds of different things that make me nervous. I'm glad to know You always love me, You're always with me, and You're always my strength. Thank You! I love You, too! Amen.

HELP FOR BROKEN HEARTS

He heals the brokenhearted and bandages their wounds.

Psalm 147:3 NLT

If you've ever felt like your heart is breaking from disappointment or betrayal or the death of someone you love, I'm so sorry. I hurt for you because I know what that is like. Please don't ever think that God has left you when you're hurting, though. He has promised that He will never leave you (Hebrews 13:5) and that He is near to the brokenhearted (Psalm 34:18) even if you don't always feel like that's true.

Maybe you just can't understand how or why awful things happen to good people. I get it. I've had those same thoughts and questions, and it's okay to tell them to God. He wants you to tell Him every worry and question you have (1 Peter 5:7). In the moments of heartbreak and questioning God, you have a choice to turn away from Him because you're mad, or you can choose to draw closer to Him and trust Him despite your hurt and anger and confusion—and let Him comfort you and help you through the dark, sad days. Little by little they *will* get better. His Word says, "Come close to God, and God will come close to you" (James 4:8 NLT).

When life is at its worst, the worst thing you can do is run from God. If you stick it out and stay close to Him, He will carry you through it.

Dear God, when I'm hurting and confused, please remind me to come closer to You, not get farther away. Only You can truly heal a broken heart. Amen.

BEST KIND OF TEST

*"When he tests me, I will come out as pure as gold.
For I have stayed on God's paths."*
JOB 23:10–11 NLT

More important than any test you take for school are the tests you take that show your faith. The Bible is clear that you will go through hard things, but there is a purpose to them. They prove whether you really believe in God and love Him. There are plenty of people in the world who say they love and follow God, but unless their lives show it through hard things, they aren't telling the truth. Read the following scripture and take heart that any hard thing you go through in life is an opportunity to keep proving that your faith is real and sharing it with others who need to know Jesus, too.

> *God has something stored up for you in heaven, where it will never decay or be ruined or disappear. You have faith in God, whose power will protect you until the last day. Then he will save you, just as he has always planned to do. On that day you will be glad, even if you have to go through many hard trials for a while. Your faith will be like gold that has been tested in a fire. And these trials will prove that your faith is worth much more than gold that can be destroyed. They will show that you will be given praise and honor and glory when Jesus Christ returns.* 1 PETER 1:4–7 CEV

*Dear God, even when I'm going through something so hard,
I want to show that my faith in You is for real.
Please help me succeed through life's tests. Amen.*

GOTTA GET YOUR REST

God rested from all his work that he had done in creation.

GENESIS 2:3 ESV

I remember being at summer camp one year in junior high and thinking it was so ridiculous and annoying that we had to take rest times in the middle of the day. Nowadays, I love naps! Whether you do or not, it's important to realize God gave us rest. It's a much-needed gift from Him. He knows we are human (He made us, so *obviously*! ☺) and our bodies have to have rest to function well and to serve Him through the great things He has planned for us to do.

It's hard to get the rest we need sometimes. Life fights us on this like crazy, with so much work to do and so many activities and people demanding our attention! But it's a battle worth fighting to get good rest. Even in one of the Ten Commandments, God commanded us to rest! Exodus 34:21 (ESV) says, " 'Six days you shall work, but on the seventh day you shall rest.' "

In the New Testament, Jesus knew He and His disciples needed rest from all the work and ministry they were doing. He says in Mark 6:31 (NLT), "Let's go off by ourselves to a quiet place and rest awhile."

It's important to remember, too, that resting and quietness is how we best come before God to remember who He is and let Him speak to us. Psalm 46:10 (ESV) says, " 'Be still, and know that I am God.' "

Dear God, please help me to realize how important good rest is. Amen.

MONEY MATTERS

Honor the Lord by giving him your money and the first part of all your crops. Then you will have more grain and grapes than you will ever need.

Proverbs 3:9–10 CEV

Are you a saver or a spender? Do you love to shop or think it's boring? Whatever the case, it's super smart to start learning to manage your money well when you're young. Don't blow it all in one place on things that don't last, and don't forget to give generously back to God. The Bible offers the most important money advice you could ever have: Jesus said, "Give, and you will receive. Your gift will return to you in full—pressed down, shaken together to make room for more, running over, and poured into your lap. The amount you give will determine the amount you get back" (Luke 6:38 NLT).

And 2 Corinthians 9:6–8 (NLT) says, "Remember this—a farmer who plants only a few seeds will get a small crop. But the one who plants generously will get a generous crop. You must each decide in your heart how much to give. And don't give reluctantly or in response to pressure. 'For God loves a person who gives cheerfully.' And God will generously provide all you need."

Dear God, please give me wisdom about money, and help me to be generous. Amen.

CONTENTMENT, NOT COMPARING

It's healthy to be content, but envy can eat you up.
PROVERBS 14:30 CEV

Want to know a way to ruin pretty much every single day of your life? Wait, what? Who wants that? Nobody! LOL!

Here's what you *don't* do if you'd rather not ruin your day—don't compare yourself or your life with others. Comparing just leads to envy or jealousy, wishing you had something that someone else does and you don't.

Instead, be content with what you have. First Timothy 6:6–8 (NLT) says, "True godliness with contentment is itself great wealth. After all, we brought nothing with us when we came into the world, and we can't take anything with us when we leave it. So if we have enough food and clothing, let us be content."

It's as simple as that. If you have food and clothing, then be content and trust that God will provide anything else you need.

Dear God, it's so hard not to look around me and see if I have what others have because I want to fit in. Please help me to focus on You and all the basic needs You provide for me. I'm grateful, and I know You will keep providing. Amen.

BOREDOM BUSTER

Take a lesson from the ants, you lazybones.
Learn from their ways and become wise!
PROVERBS 6:6 NLT

As God grows you to be a girl of grace, you'll find it's hard to ever be bored, and that's a good thing! Boredom is often related to laziness, and God's Word tells us very strongly *not* to be lazy. Check it out:

> *Lazy people want much but get little, but those who work hard will prosper.* PROVERBS 13:4 NLT
>
> *"The one who is unwilling to work shall not eat."* 2 THESSALONIANS 3:10 NIV
>
> *Lazy people are soon poor; hard workers get rich.* PROVERBS 10:4 NLT
>
> *A lazy person is as bad as someone who destroys things.* PROVERBS 18:9 NLT
>
> *If you are lazy and sleep your time away, you will starve.* PROVERBS 19:15 CEV

There's always something to do to serve God and share His love! You can ask yourself the moment you start to sense that bored feeling coming over you: "What could I do right now to be productive, helpful, encouraging, and smart with my time?"

Dear God, I want to use my time wisely. Show me Your will and the good things You have planned for me to help others know Your love and grace! Amen.

NOT JUST A NICKNAME

*See what great love the Father has lavished on us,
that we should be called children of God!
And that is what we are!*

1 John 3:1 NIV

Maybe you have a family member or friend who calls you Princess as a nickname. But if you've asked Jesus to be your Savior, you can totally *own* that name! He is the King of all kings and Lord of all lords (Revelation 17:14; 19:16), and John 1 says about Jesus, "The Word was in the world, but no one knew him, though God had made the world with his Word. He came into his own world, but his own nation did not welcome him. Yet some people accepted him and put their faith in him. So he gave them the right to be the children of God. They were not God's children by nature or because of any human desires. God himself was the one who made them his children" (vv. 10–13 CEV).

So, truly you are royalty, my princess friend! Now, don't let that go to your head and start demanding service from others and a fancy new wardrobe and such! Our King is both sovereign and almighty yet a humble servant of others.

Dear God, I am amazed that You offer anyone who believes in You the right to be Your child! Thank You for letting me be Your princess! Amen.

MORE ABOUT YOUR ROYALTY

"For the Lord your God is the God of gods and Lord of lords. He is the great God, the mighty and awesome God."

Deuteronomy 10:17 NLT

You truly are a princess if you trust Jesus as your Savior, but Jesus set the example of a loving and humble Lord of all lords, and you are called to be like Him (1 John 2:3–6). Philippians 2:3–7 (NLT) says, "Be humble, thinking of others as better than yourselves. Don't look out only for your own interests, but take an interest in others, too. You must have the same attitude that Christ Jesus had. Though he was God, he did not think of equality with God as something to cling to. Instead, he gave up his divine privileges."

It was after Jesus had given up everything in order to save others that God lifted Him to "the place of highest honor and gave him the name above all other names, that at the name of Jesus every knee should bow, in heaven and on earth and under the earth, and every tongue declare that Jesus Christ is Lord, to the glory of God the Father" (Philippians 2:9–11 NLT).

Your life will not be exactly like Jesus', of course, but you are called to copy Him. He did not expect to be honored like royalty here on earth, and neither should you. Instead, you are called to give that honor up and serve people and share the love of the Gospel so that others will believe in Jesus, too. Then, for eternity someday, you will receive your forever reward of living in a perfect kingdom for all of God's children!

Dear Jesus, I want to have confidence that I am Your princess, but I want to serve others with humility like You did. Please help me. Amen.

GOD'S GREAT FAITHFULNESS

God is faithful, by whom you were called into the fellowship of his Son, Jesus Christ our Lord.
1 CORINTHIANS 1:9 ESV

If you've ever had a good friendship come to an end, you know how hard it is to lose someone who you thought was faithful. In those hard times, you can be thankful that God is *always* faithful. People make mistakes and will disappoint you, but God's faithfulness is endless.

When you feel let down by someone, focus on these scriptures that describe the great faithfulness of God:

> *Those who know your name trust in you, for you, LORD, have never forsaken those who seek you.* PSALM 9:10 NIV
>
> *But the Lord is faithful, and he will strengthen you and protect you from the evil one.* 2 THESSALONIANS 3:3 NIV
>
> *If we are unfaithful, he remains faithful, for he cannot deny who he is.* 2 TIMOTHY 2:13 NLT
>
> *"God is not a man, so he does not lie. He is not human, so he does not change his mind. Has he ever spoken and failed to act? Has he ever promised and not carried it through?"* NUMBERS 23:19 NLT

Dear God, Your faithfulness amazes me. I'm so grateful I can count on You no matter what is going on or who lets me down. Amen.

LOVE YOUR LEADERS

Remember your leaders, those who spoke to you the word of God. Consider the outcome of their way of life, and imitate their faith.

HEBREWS 13:7 ESV

When you're young, you have a lot of leaders in your life—pastors and teachers at your church, teachers and leaders at school, coaches and instructors of your sports teams and activities, and especially your older family members like Mom and Dad, grandparents, aunts, uncles, and others.

I know it sometimes feels like they're all just bossing you around or giving you advice you don't need, but next time you're feeling frustrated, take a different approach. Think about how they're trying to help you learn and grow and make good decisions. Thank God for them, even if in the moment you're not feeling very happy with their instructions because you just want to do your own thing. I remember those feelings when I was a girl, and now that I'm a grown-up, I can look back with deep appreciation for all the people who helped teach and guide me—especially my mom who is gone to heaven now. I wish so badly I could still ask her for advice.

Hebrews 13:17 (NLT) says, "Obey your spiritual leaders, and do what they say. Their work is to watch over your souls, and they are accountable to God. Give them reason to do this with joy and not with sorrow."

Dear God, please help me to appreciate and accept leadership from the good people who love You and who are in authority over me, especially my parents. Amen.

HONOR YOUR PARENTS

"Honor your father and your mother, that your days may be long in the land that the Lord your God is giving you."

Exodus 20:12 ESV

Not only are you to obey your parents, you are to honor them. That means not just doing what they ask but doing it with a good attitude. You shouldn't grumble and complain as you obey. Appreciate them and respect them and tell them you love them, no matter what's going on in your family. That's a great way to honor them.

As you grow older and eventually become an adult, you will make your own decisions and rules, but you can still honor and bless your parents by maintaining a great relationship with them and spending time with them, even if you don't live close by. With all the forms of communication these days—texting, phone calls, e-mail, FaceTime and Skype, and of course good old-fashioned snail mail—this is not hard. You can keep asking them for advice and to share the wisdom they've gained over the many more years of living they've done than you.

Dear God, please help me to honor and obey my parents now, and when I'm an adult, please help me to continue to have good relationships with them. I thank You for my good parents, God! I love You and I love them! Amen.

BE A LEADER

In everything set them an example by doing what is good.

Titus 2:7 niv

If you're able to read this book, then you're able to be a leader, too. Because if you're at an age when you can read, then you're at an age when you can be a helper to those younger than you, and that makes you a leader and example to others. Jodi and Lilly have been helping me in Sunday school class at church since they were each about four years old. They started helping in the two-and-three-year-olds' class with simple things like passing out cups and napkins at snack time and modeling good behavior like sharing and patiently waiting for their turn. As they've gotten older they help make up game ideas to keep younger kids occupied, comfort little ones who miss their parents, and read books to little kiddos.

Always remember that you are not too young to be a leader yourself! Live your life according to God's Word, always looking for ways to serve and help others and share your faith. That's the best kind of leader in a world that so desperately needs God's truth and love.

Dear Jesus, please show me how to be the kind of servant-leader You want me to be, to help others know You as their Savior, too. Amen.

GOD MAKES THINGS NEW

And the one sitting on the throne said,
"Look, I am making everything new!"
REVELATION 21:5 NLT

We recently saw the movie *Smurfs: The Lost Village*, and it was so fun! I love when movie producers do a good job of bringing back an old favorite from my childhood in a new way that I can enjoy with Jodi and Lilly. Some remakes are great, and some not so much.

I'm thankful that all of God's remakes are perfect! His grace takes people who were once lost in their sin and turns them into completely new people. Second Corinthians 5:17 (NLT) says, "Anyone who belongs to Christ has become a new person. The old life is gone; a new life has begun!"

Anytime you find yourself headed down a wrong path for a bit, making bad choices or keeping a bad attitude, God's grace can quickly help you turn around and away from sin. Pray this prayer from Psalm 51:10 (NLT): "Create in me a clean heart, O God. Renew a loyal spirit within me."

And remember and trust that God's mercies "begin afresh each morning" (Lamentations 3:23 NLT). Each new day is a day to let God do something new in you!

Dear God, thank You for all You have done and all You are doing to make things new and perfect! Amen.

HAVING GREAT GRATITUDE

Be thankful in all circumstances, for this is God's will for you who belong to Christ Jesus.
1 THESSALONIANS 5:18 NLT

A girl of grace is a girl who is full of gratitude. You can find a reason to give thanks in any situation. Yes, even when your siblings are driving you crazy. Even when your homework seems ridiculously hard. Even when a family situation is completely out of control. Even when someone you love dies. Even during the worst kinds of situations, you can simply thank God that He is with you and hears you. Thank Him for being a good and loving heavenly Father! Then ask Him to help you focus on the blessings you have in the moment, even if it's simply the ability to take a big deep breath and pray some more. As you continue to trust in God and thank Him for what He does, He will show you more reasons to have gratitude.

Read and remember these scriptures, and make them your goal:

> *Let all that I am praise the LORD; may I never forget the good things he does for me.* PSALM 103:2 NLT

> *Give thanks to the LORD and proclaim his greatness. Let the whole world know what he has done.*
> 1 CHRONICLES 16:8 NLT

> *And give thanks for everything to God the Father in the name of our Lord Jesus Christ.* EPHESIANS 5:20 NLT

Dear God, I thank You for who You are and for all of the blessings in my life. Please grow me in grace and in gratitude. Amen.

THROUGH EVERY AWFUL THING

"When you pass through the waters, I will be with you; and through the rivers, they shall not overwhelm you; when you walk through fire you shall not be burned, and the flame shall not consume you."

Isaiah 43:2 ESV

God has never promised anyone a constantly comfortable life. There is no easy-peasy path through this world because sin messed up all the goodness God intended for His creation. But through Jesus Christ, God is working out His plan to defeat sin forever, and in the meantime, He does promise to be with you through every hard thing you go through, like Isaiah 43:2 describes. This scripture makes me think of the cool Old Testament stories of Shadrach, Meshach, and Abednego who were literally put into a fiery furnace but did not burn up. Read their story in Daniel 3, especially the awesomeness that after being in the furnace (spoiler alert!), "not a hair on their heads was singed, and their clothing was not scorched. They didn't even smell of smoke!" (v. 27 NLT).

God didn't keep Daniel from being put in the terrifying lions' den, either, but He did protect him through it: "Not a scratch was found on him, for he had trusted in his God" (Daniel 6:23 NLT).

When you're in the middle of something scary or painful, remember these Old Testament heroes whom God used to show how He is right beside us holding us through every hard thing.

Dear God, please don't ever let me forget how close You are at all times, in every situation. You've never promised to keep me out of all pain and trouble, but You've promised to always help me through it. Amen.

TURN PAIN INTO PRAISE

You have turned my mourning into joyful dancing.
Psalm 30:11 NLT

The hardest, most hurtful thing Jodi, Lilly, and I have experienced so far in our lives is the sudden death of my mom and their dear nana. We had such a close relationship with her and shared so much love. We're grateful for all the good memories and all the dear family and friends we still have with us, but it still hurts so bad to have lost her here. We can only focus on God's truth and His promises that everyone who trusts Him as Savior has eternal life with Him in heaven. So we know without a doubt that that's where our mom and nana is now, just waiting till it's our turn to be there, too.

God is so close to us in the midst of our pain of missing her. A dear friend reminded us that the best thing to do when the pain hurts the worst is to praise God. It seems impossible at first, but truly, we have found that is the best remedy and comfort for the pain. Focusing our thoughts on who God is and how awesome He is eases the intense pain every single time because it reminds us of His truth and His love and His good plans for a perfect forever for all who love Him!

So, friends, when you are hurting for any reason, remember to let the pain cause you to praise God. Read the psalms, and sing praise and worship songs to Him!

Dear God, please help me to praise You in every painful situation. Amen.

OUR RACE

You know that many runners enter a race, and only one of them wins the prize. So run to win! Athletes work hard to win a crown that cannot last, but we do it for a crown that will last forever.

1 Corinthians 9:24–25 CEV

Maybe you've heard that joke that goes something like this: "I don't run. And if you ever see me running, you should run, too, because something is probably chasing me." Haha! It makes me laugh every time because it's so true for me. I used to jog with friends in college, and that was fun—but I'd much prefer getting some exercise taking a long walk around my neighborhood or preferably on a beach!

What's your favorite kind of exercise? Even though I don't run, I love the inspiring examples of running that scripture gives us for helping us stay strong in our faith in Jesus through our journey of life: "Such a large crowd of witnesses is all around us! So we must get rid of everything that slows us down, especially the sin that just won't let go. And we must be determined to run the race that is ahead of us. We must keep our eyes on Jesus, who leads us and makes our faith complete. He endured the shame of being nailed to a cross, because he knew that later on he would be glad he did. Now he is seated at the right side of God's throne! So keep your mind on Jesus, who put up with many insults from sinners. Then you won't get discouraged and give up" (Hebrews 12:1–3 CEV).

Dear God, when my journey through life feels so difficult and I want to give up, please help me keep my eyes on You and keep running with You and toward heaven. Amen.

THE LEAST OF THESE

"The righteous will answer him, 'Lord, when did we see you hungry and feed you, or thirsty and give you something to drink? When did we see you a stranger and invite you in, or needing clothes and clothe you? When did we see you sick or in prison and go to visit you?' The King will reply, 'Truly I tell you, whatever you did for one of the least of these brothers and sisters of mine, you did for me.' "

MATTHEW 25:37–40 NIV

Growing up, I spent a lot of time with elderly people in an assisted-living home where my mom worked as a nurse. I also visited people in a nursing home every week when I was in college. Now I'm glad Jodi and Lilly spend lots of time with their grandma and great-grandma at a nursing home. They often play bingo together, and just their presence is an encouragement to the elderly people who need visitors and to see life and the joy of young people in their sometimes dreary days as they struggle with health problems.

Too often, our world doesn't put much value on elderly people because, as their bodies age, they can't seem to do much anymore. But they are so valuable. Every life is priceless to God, and those who are older have much wisdom to share. In caring about them and for them, we are doing what Jesus described in saying, "Whatever you did for one of the least of these brothers and sisters of mine, you did for me."

Dear God, help me to care about and show love to others who seem less important in our world. Amen.

NO MORE BLACK-AND-BLUE

For his unfailing love toward those who fear him is as great as the height of the heavens above the earth. He has removed our sins as far from us as the east is from the west.

PSALM 103:11–12 NLT

It's frustrating to struggle with the same kind of mistake again and again. We all have areas like this that vex us! Even the apostle Paul said, "I want to do what is right, but I can't. I want to do what is good, but I don't. I don't want to do what is wrong, but I do it anyway" (Romans 7:18–19 NLT).

Our enemy, Satan, wants us to keep beating ourselves up over everything we struggle with. Because if we keep focusing on what we do *wrong*, we'll never realize all the *right* and awesome things God wants to do through us, all the blessings He wants to give us, too! Don't let Satan convince you to beat yourself black-and-blue over your mistakes. Trust God's Word and His grace! First John 1:9 (NIV) says, "If we confess our sins, he is faithful and just and will forgive us our sins and purify us from all unrighteousness."

So when you mess up, admit it to God and make it right with others who might be involved. Ask for forgiveness and then trust that God takes that sin as far away from you as the east is from the west! Honestly, you're going to have to repeat this process like a zillion times in your life, but that's why we need God so much, and why His endless grace is such an incredible blessing!

Dear God, please help me to confess my wrongs, ask for forgiveness, and then let You shower me with Your grace as I move forward into the right things You have for me. Amen.

PUTTING ON GOD'S ARMOR

Be strong in the Lord and in his mighty power. Put on all of God's armor so that you will be able to stand firm against all strategies of the devil.

Ephesians 6:10–11 NLT

When Jodi and Lilly were younger, we enjoyed reading from a fun princess storybook that told a story of a girl who dressed up like a knight so she could joust like her brother. Girls weren't allowed, but no one knew it was her under all that protective armor. In the end, she proved everyone wrong and showed that a girl could joust and win!

In your real-life story, you need armor, too, but not for jousting on horses. You need the armor of God to battle the enemies who are constantly fighting against anyone who loves Jesus.

Ephesians 6:12–13 (NLT) says, "For we are not fighting against flesh-and-blood enemies, but against evil rulers and authorities of the unseen world, against mighty powers in this dark world, and against evil spirits in the heavenly places. Therefore, put on every piece of God's armor so you will be able to resist the enemy in the time of evil. Then after the battle you will still be standing firm."

Dear God, please help me to learn more about Your mighty armor and how to use it to protect against my unseen enemies. Amen.

EACH PIECE OF GOD'S ARMOR, PART 1

Therefore, put on every piece of God's armor so you will be able to resist the enemy in the time of evil. Then after the battle you will still be standing firm. Stand your ground, putting on the belt of truth and the body armor of God's righteousness. For shoes, put on the peace that comes from the Good News so that you will be fully prepared.

Ephesians 6:13–15 NLT

Every morning when you're getting dressed and brushing your hair and teeth, you'd be super smart to ask God to help you make sure every piece of His armor fits just right for whatever the day holds. He gives you a belt of truth, which holds everything together by knowing all truth comes from God who is Truth. He gives you the body armor of righteousness that protects your heart and soul from any evil with the righteousness that can only come by the grace of Jesus Christ. He gives you shoes that both protect your feet and equip you to carry the Gospel to others.

Almighty God, please help me remember every day to picture my spiritual armor and put it on with Your help. I'm ready to fight my spiritual enemies who want to drag me away from You. Amen.

EACH PIECE OF GOD'S ARMOR, PART 2

In addition to all of these, hold up the shield of faith to stop the fiery arrows of the devil. Put on salvation as your helmet, and take the sword of the Spirit, which is the word of God.

EPHESIANS 6:16–17 NLT

God also gives you a shield of faith in Him that protects you from all the weapons and tricky things that Satan and his spiritual armies will throw at you. God gives you a helmet of salvation that protects your head and mind, helping you to trust that no matter what happens here on earth, you are saved for an eternal life forever in heaven. And God gives you an awesome weapon to fight your unseen enemies with—the sword of the Spirit, which is the Word of God.

Don't feel silly every morning, asking God to help you put this armor on. Instead, trust that God's Word is true and that you need this armor. It's not just pretend. Let God empower you like only He can.

Almighty God, I'm so thankful that in a dark world that has so much evil, You have not left me to fight alone. You have given me everything I need to fight against evil with good and to help others know Your truth and love. Amen.

KNOWING YOUR BIBLE WELL

Your word is a lamp to guide my feet and a light for my path.
Psalm 119:105 NLT

I remember doing sword drills at church during vacation Bible school when I was little. A leader would call out a scripture reference, and the first to find it in their Bible would win the race! Being fast is not the important part, though; it's simply so important to know your Bible well as God is growing you to be a girl of grace. God's Word is a living and active book, and it's how He speaks best to us. The more you know about it, the closer you can grow to God, the better able you are to navigate through any situation of life, and the better you can give answers to others for the faith that you have (1 Peter 3:15) and the help that they might need.

If you want a fun way to start learning a whole overview of the Bible, I'd encourage you to watch the What's in the Bible series of movies. There's a whole set that digs in briefly, in fun and interesting ways, through every book of the Bible to teach you more about it!

Dear God, please grow in me a strong desire to know Your Word, the Holy Bible, well. Please guide me through it, and draw me closer to You! Amen.

CHRISTIANS AROUND THE WORLD

Pray in the Spirit at all times and on every occasion.
Stay alert and be persistent in your prayers
for all believers everywhere.

Ephesians 6:18 NLT

It is no small blessing that we did much of the brainstorming and writing of this book in public places like coffee shops. Did you know that in many countries around the world, there is no way we could have done that? It would not have been safe to openly talk about the one true God and our Savior Jesus Christ, with a Bible open for anyone to see.

I'm extremely grateful for the freedom of religion that we have in the U.S., and I hope you are, too. I hope you're also constantly aware of the believers all around the world who do not have freedom like we do but who risk their safety and their lives every day to keep living for Jesus. I'm so amazed and inspired by the way they let God give them incredible courage to spread His truth in dangerous places. Ephesians 6:18 reminds me to pray for them and all others like them at all times. Will you join me?

Dear God, thank You for my freedoms and protections. I pray that You will also provide freedom and protection for all the Christians around the world who live in places where it is dangerous to believe in You. Amen.

SWEET TEETH AND SELF-CONTROL

For God gave us a spirit not of fear
but of power and love and self-control.
2 Timothy 1:7 esv

I don't think I have just one sweet tooth; I think maybe every tooth in my mouth is a sweet tooth! I love chocolate and cookies and doughnuts and all those yummy things. It's so hard not to eat too much of them! Sweets are an area where I could use a lot more self-control.

Self-control is so important for all areas of life. We can't just say any thought that pops into our head whenever we want to. . . . We can't act on any and every desire we have. . . . We can't always just play or go on vacation. . . . You get the idea! We have to watch our words; we have to act with both the present and the future in mind and knowing our actions affect others, too; and we have to do the work and chores and lessons that are required in life. Self-control is incredibly important!

Proverbs 25:28 (nlt) says, "A person without self-control is like a city with broken-down walls." In other words, a person without self-control is in chaos and ruin. Ask God every day to give you more self-control, through His power, so that you live a successful life according to His will!

Dear God, please increase self-control in me, and help me to live the best kind of life that pleases You and gives You glory! Amen.

TOTALLY RANDOM

I urge, then, first of all, that petitions, prayers, intercession and thanksgiving be made for all people.
1 Timothy 2:1 NIV

On a shopping trip for Easter dresses one year, Jodi, Lilly, and I were stopped by an older woman who asked if she could walk with us out to the parking lot. She was struggling with anxiety, feeling scared and worried, which she said often happened to her in big busy places. I could tell she was sincere, so we walked her to her car, and then I asked her if she needed anything else or if I could call anyone for her. She assured me she was fine and would be okay to drive home. Then, even though it made me nervous, I asked if I could pray out loud for her. She agreed, and with a simple, short prayer I asked God to bless her and keep her safe.

Jodi and Lilly still talk about that experience sometimes, just how random it was but also good that we could help and pray for a stranger. I was blessed to be able to pray for her and hopefully encourage her and share a bit of God's love.

When you feel the Holy Spirit leading you, don't be afraid to boldly ask if you can pray for someone, especially someone who does not know Jesus. You never can tell how God is going to use those prayers!

Dear God, please help me to be bold in a good way in praying for others. Amen.

KEEPING SANE WITH SOCIAL MEDIA

Look carefully then how you walk, not as unwise but as wise, making the best use of the time, because the days are evil. Therefore do not be foolish, but understand what the will of the Lord is.

EPHESIANS 5:15–17 ESV

I love social media. It's wonderful to stay connected with friends and family all over the country and world, and you've probably seen some of the hilarious things out there that are just for fun like crazy cat videos and babies doing adorably funny stuff.

But in some ways I find social media a frustrating struggle because it's tempting to spend way too much time on my smartphone reading posts and blogs and tweets and such. It's also hard to avoid some of the harmful stuff that's out there everywhere on the Internet, things that do not help us focus on "whatever is true, whatever is noble, whatever is right, whatever is pure, whatever is lovely, whatever is admirable" (Philippians 4:8 NIV).

Whether you're into it much yet or not, as you get older you'll realize our world revolves a lot around social media. There's a lot of good about that but a lot of bad, too. Pray for wisdom from God to help you use social media wisely and spend your time on it wisely.

Dear God, I want to start now making good use of my time and being smart about social media. Please give me Your wisdom. Amen.

NO MORE IDOLS

Jesus told him. "For the Scriptures say, 'You must worship the LORD your God and serve only him.' "

MATTHEW 4:10 NLT

When you hear the word *idol*, do you think of some big stone statue in ancient times that people bowed down to? Or maybe you think of the golden calf that the Israelites created out of their jewelry when they were tired of waiting on God and Moses (Exodus 32).

It may seem ridiculous to those of us who love Jesus to think it possible to have an idol. Why would anyone worship some object made of metal or stone that just sits there and does nothing, right? But did you know that idols can actually be anything that we put above God on our list of priorities?

- Your family and friends can be idols if they come before your relationship with God.
- Your schoolwork can be an idol if it's your only goal and focus in life.
- Your smartphone and social media accounts can be idols if they take up all your attention.
- Your sports and activities can be idols if they're your only purpose in life.

God wants us to focus on Him first in our lives and then let all those other things fall into place in the correct order below Him on the list. When He is first, He helps us succeed the best ways possible in everything else.

Dear God, please help me put You on the very top of my priority list. I want to spend time with You and I thank You for the way everything else will fall into place just right when I do. Amen.

BUILDING UP

We should help others do what is right and build them up in the Lord.
ROMANS 15:2 NLT

When you're young, you might not feel like you can do much for God since you still have so much to learn. But the best way to learn about God and how to live life is to serve God now while you also keep reading His Word. And one of the best ways that any young person can serve God now is to encourage others like scripture tells us to. With simply a cheerful attitude and joyful smile, you can spread encouragement. With a phone call or text to let a friend know you are thinking of them, you can build someone else up. You can share hugs, scriptures, and prayer for others who are in need or who simply could use an extra bright spot in their day. Read these scriptures and ask God to help you be encouraging to others every single day.

So encourage each other and build each other up, just as you are already doing. 1 THESSALONIANS 5:11 NLT

Let everything you say be good and helpful, so that your words will be an encouragement to those who hear them. EPHESIANS 4:29 NLT

Dear God, please remind me constantly how easy it is to encourage others and lift their spirits. Show me whom You want me to encourage today. Amen.

HOLD ON!

Let us hold tightly without wavering to the hope we affirm, for God can be trusted to keep his promise. Let us think of ways to motivate one another to acts of love and good works. And let us not neglect our meeting together, as some people do, but encourage one another, especially now that the day of his return is drawing near.

Hebrews 10:23–25 NLT

You've probably seen a movie or TV show where the bad guy is trying to push or pry the hands of the good guy off the edge of a cliff or building or something so he'll fall. You can think of Satan and our enemies in this world like those bad guys—always trying to pry your fingers off your Bible, always trying to get you to let go of your faith and hope and your desire to follow God.

The bad guys will do anything at all to make you fall away from your hope in God. That's why Hebrews 10:23–25 is so important to remember. We must hold tightly to our hope in God, trusting that He keeps His promises, and encourage each other to continue sharing love and good deeds. And we need to go to church regularly with fellow believers so that we can worship God together. God is coming back soon, and we just have to hold on tight until that great day!

Dear God, I don't ever want to let go of my awesome hope in You! Please help me to hold on so tightly! Amen.

THE RIGHT WAY TO BRAG

This is what the Lord says: "Let not the wise boast of their wisdom or the strong boast of their strength or the rich boast of their riches, but let the one who boasts boast about this: that they have the understanding to know me, that I am the Lord, who exercises kindness, justice and righteousness on earth, for in these I delight," declares the Lord.

Jeremiah 9:23–24 niv

If you know anyone who brags or boasts all the time, you know how annoying that can be. It's wonderful to share exciting, happy news with friends and be excited together. It's just not kind or polite for anyone to constantly try to show off why their blessings and accomplishments and plans are better than yours.

Here's how you can brag and feel good about it:

- ***Don't*** brag about your plans: When making your plans, you should not brag about them but acknowledge that "what you ought to say is, 'If the Lord wants us to, we will live and do this or that.' Otherwise you are boasting about your own pretentious plans, and all such boasting is evil" (James 4:15–16 nlt). And Proverbs 27:1 (niv) says, "Do not boast about tomorrow, for you do not know what a day may bring."
- **Do** brag about God and His love for us through Jesus Christ! Galatians 6:14 (nlt) says, "As for me, may I never boast about anything except the cross of our Lord Jesus Christ."

Dear God, please help me not to brag about anything but You and Your love and power! Amen.

KEEP THE LIGHTS ON

"For all that is secret will eventually be brought into the open, and everything that is concealed will be brought to light and made known to all."

Luke 8:17 NLT

Secrets are so fun when they're for a good reason—a surprise birthday party, the Christmas gift you can't wait to give, or a big chore you got done around the house like a ninja to help out.

But secrets that you keep because you don't want to tell the truth are usually not okay. And trying to keep a secret from God is never a good idea, not to mention silly since He already knows it anyway. Psalm 44:21 (NLT) says, "God would surely have known it, for he knows the secrets of every heart."

You don't have to always tell every person your every thought; in fact, that's not a good idea at all. But just remember that God hears and knows. Don't ever try to hide anything from Him. Keep an honest, close relationship with God, through the grace of Jesus, and talk to Him about everything. How amazing that the God of all the universe wants you to! If you keep everything in good communication with God, you'll never have to worry about anything hiding in the dark that will be brought out into the light.

Dear God, You are always with me and I can't keep any secrets from You. Please help me never want to. You are so good and loving, and I'm thankful You want me to live in light, not darkness. Amen.

FLEE!

And give no opportunity to the devil.
Ephesians 4:27 ESV

You have quite a challenge ahead of you, growing up in a world that tries to tell girls all kinds of things that are drastically opposite of God's good guidelines in His Word—guidelines that are just meant to protect you and help you live the best life possible. So please, friends, get it in your head now that the Bible talks a lot about FLEEING any situation and experience you're faced with that gives you opportunity to sin (1 Timothy 6:11–12; 2 Timothy 2:22; 1 Corinthians 6:18). Don't mess around with situations you sense the Holy Spirit saying are not good for you, telling yourself, "I just want to do what my friends are doing and this won't hurt me. I've got this under control. I'll just watch and not participate. . .or maybe just a little. . . ." No! The Bible doesn't say you should hang around on the edges of sinful situations. You should run away from them—fast and hard, like the word *flee* expresses.

Yes, you might lose friends this way. And you will be A-OK if you do! I promise you, you do not want those kinds of friends in your life anyway. Any friend who will not respect your beliefs and convictions is not a true friend and never has been. They will only tear you down and away from the best life God wants for you. You can trust that God will bless you time and time again when you obey Him and flee from situations and friendships that tempt you into trouble.

Dear God, please give me courage and wisdom to know when to flee situations that will cause me to sin. I trust that You always want what is best for me, and I want to obey Your Word. Amen.

TRUTH VS. FEELINGS

The sum of your word is truth.
PSALM 119:160 ESV

In general, we girls have pretty strong emotions. All of us show and feel them in different ways, but I think we can all agree how crazy-powerful they seem at times. And they're so fickle (meaning they change a lot), right? That's why it's extremely important to learn that truth is always, always, always more important than your feelings.

For example, you will have times when you don't feel like being a Christian, when it would be easier to just be like the world, but here's truth from God's Word that helps control those feelings: "Do not love this world nor the things it offers you, for when you love the world, you do not have the love of the Father in you. For the world offers only a craving for physical pleasure, a craving for everything we see, and pride in our achievements and possessions. These are not from the Father, but are from this world. And this world is fading away, along with everything that people crave. But anyone who does what pleases God will live forever" (1 John 2:15–17 NLT).

When your feelings might be overtaking you, remind yourself in all situations to slow down, take deep breaths, and think about what is true. No matter how strong your feelings are, they will lie to you sometimes. The truth is what beats feelings. And the truth is always found in God's Word.

Dear God, please help me to keep my feelings in check and focus mostly on Your truth. Amen.

UTMOST BLISS

One day as he saw the crowds gathering, Jesus went up on the mountainside and sat down. His disciples gathered around him, and he began to teach them.

Matthew 5:1–2 NLT

One of my favorite passages of scripture is the Beatitudes of Jesus. *Beatitude* is another word for blessing, and the Merriam-Webster dictionary describes it as "a state of utmost bliss." Truly, when we follow these words of Jesus, we will experience utmost bliss both now and forever in heaven!

> *"God blesses those who are poor and realize their need for him, for the Kingdom of Heaven is theirs. God blesses those who mourn, for they will be comforted. God blesses those who are humble, for they will inherit the whole earth. God blesses those who hunger and thirst for justice, for they will be satisfied. God blesses those who are merciful, for they will be shown mercy. God blesses those whose hearts are pure, for they will see God. God blesses those who work for peace, for they will be called the children of God. God blesses those who are persecuted for doing right, for the Kingdom of Heaven is theirs. God blesses you when people mock you and persecute you and lie about you and say all sorts of evil things against you because you are my followers. Be happy about it! Be very glad! For a great reward awaits you in heaven."* Matthew 5:3–12 NLT

Dear Jesus, please help me to follow Your teaching in the Beatitudes. I want to be blessed for doing what is good according to You! Amen.

WHEN LIFE IS SO CONFUSING

Oh, how great are God's riches and wisdom and knowledge! How impossible it is for us to understand his decisions and his ways!

ROMANS 11:33 NLT

Here we are at the end, and I sure hope this book has helped you grow in the awesome grace of Jesus! I know life still feels super confusing sometimes. Living as a Christian in this crazy world seems like you always have to go against the flow. Some people say the Bible is too old and doesn't matter anymore. Sometimes the Bible *does* seem confusing and disconnected to the present, but don't get discouraged. Keep following God and trusting Him to show you what you need and what to do. You will never figure out everything about this life and about God here on earth, and that's okay! First Corinthians 13:12 (NLT) says, "Now we see things imperfectly, like puzzling reflections in a mirror, but then we will see everything with perfect clarity. All that I know now is partial and incomplete, but then I will know everything completely, just as God now knows me completely."

Each new day, keep following God, one step at a time, through His Spirit and His Word, praying to Him constantly. If you get off track, simply ask for forgiveness and come back to Him! His grace is endless—and remember, He wants to shower you with it! Never forget that your reward for following Him is beyond anything you can ever dream of, for " 'no eye has seen, no ear has heard, and no mind has imagined what God has prepared for those who love him' " (1 Corinthians 2:9 NLT).

Dear God, I don't understand everything about You, but I want to keep learning more and growing in Your amazing grace. Thank You! Amen.

SCRIPTURE INDEX